READING
COMPREHENSION
WORKSHOP
SPECTRUM

GLOBE FEARON
EDUCATIONAL PUBLISHER
PARAMUS, NEW JERSEY

Paramount Publishing

Executive Editor: Virginia Seeley
Senior Editor: Bernice Golden
Editor: Lynn W. Kloss
Editorial Assistant: Roger Weisman
Product Development: Brown Publishing Network
                       Book Production Systems
Art Director: Nancy Sharkey

Production Manager: Penny Gibson
Production Editors: Nicole Cypher, Eric Dawson
Marketing Manager: Sandra Hutchison
Photo Research: Jenifer Hixson
Electronic Page Production: Siren Design
Cover Design: Carol Anson
Cover Illustration: Jennifer Bolten

Globe Fearon Educational Publisher wishes to thank the following copyright owners for permission to reproduce copyrighted selections in this book: **The Caxton Printers Ltd., Caldwell, Idaho**, for Toshio Mori "The All-American Girl" from *Yokohama, California.* Copyright ©1949. **Dell Books, a division of Bantam Doubleday Dell Publishing Group, Inc.,** for Wilson Rawls *Where the Red Fern Grows.* Copyright (c) 1961 by Woodrow Wilson Rawls. Copyright (c) 1961 by Curtis Publishing Co. **EMI Music**, for Carole King "You've Got a Friend." (c) 1971 Colgems-EMI Music Inc. All Rights Reserved. International copyright secured. **Harrison Music Corp.**, for Bob Russell "He Ain't Heavy . . . He's My Brother" (music by Bobby Scott). Copyright (c) 1969 by Harrison Music Corp. and Jenny Music Inc. All rights reserved. **Herald Square Music, Inc.,** for Bob Thiele and George David Weiss "What a Wonderful World." (c) 1967 Range Road Music Inc., and Quartet Music Inc. All rights reserved. **Francisco Jimenez**, for Francisco Jimenez "The Circuit" from *North of the Rio Grande*, edited and with an introduction by Edward Simmen. First published in the *Arizona Quarterly* (Autumn, 1973). Copyright 1973 by Francisco Jimenez. **June Jordan**, for June Jordan "On the Spirit of Mildred Jordan" from *Things That I Do in the Dark* (New York: Random House, 1977). Copyright (c) 1970 June Jordan. **Richard E. Kim**, for "Crossing" from *Lost Names: Scenes from a Korean Boyhood.* (c) 1970, 1988 Richard E. Kim. **Latin American Literary Review Press, Pittsburgh, PA**, for Isabel Fraire "Housing Complex" from *Poems in the Lap of Death*, translated by Thomas Hoeksema. (c) 1981. **Louisiana State University Press**, for Marilyn Nelson Waniek "The Lost Daughter" from *Mama's Promises.* Copyright (c) 1985 by Marilyn Nelson Waniek. **Irma McClaurin-Allen**, for Irma McClaurin "The Power of Names" from *Pearl's Song* (Lotus Press, 1988). Copyright (c) 1988 by Irma McClaurin. All rights reserved. **The New Yorker Magazine, Inc.**, for Joseph D'O'Brian "New York City: Off the Beaten Path" from *The New Yorker* (October 4, 1993, special advertising section). (c) 1993. All rights reserved. **University of North Dakota School of Medicine, Indians into Medicine program**, for Jim Beiswenger, program specialist, "Indians into Medicine" letter to students. Globe Fearon Educational Publisher has executed a reasonable and concerted effort to contact the author or agent of the song "Por Mi Camino" by Celso Pina. Globe Fearon Educational Publisher eagerly invites any persons knowledgeable about the whereabouts of this author or agent to contact Globe Fearon Educational Publisher to arrange for the customary publishing transactions.

Globe Fearon Educational Publisher wishes to thank the following copyright owners for permission to reproduce illustrations and photographs in this book. **p.13**: Photograph, UPI/Bettmann; **p.29**: Illustration by David Tamura; **p.46**: Illustration by Siren Design; **pp. 64-66**: Photographs by Nick Smith; **p. 70**: Photograph, American Museum of Natural History; **p. 119**: Photograph, Reuters/Bettmann; **p. 125**: Photograph, The Bettmann Archive; **p. 138, 142**: Illustrations by Siren Design; **p. 141**: Photograph, Stock Boston; **p. 146**: Photograph courtesy of The Standard Oil Company.

Printed in the United States of America   4 5 6 7 8 9 10 99 98

ISBN: 0-835-90571-3

GLOBE FEARON
EDUCATIONAL PUBLISHER
PARAMUS, NEW JERSEY

Paramount Publishing

Contents

Unit ONE

BECOMING AN ACTIVE READER

Critical readers become involved while reading **autobiographical fiction.** They compare their own lives to the characters whose lives reflect real-life events. Critical readers are often moved to tears or laughter as they become involved in the characters' lives.

Using Skills and Strategies

Becoming aware of details that create a **mood** in the story will help you understand the author's message. You might ask: Which story clues help me identify the mood or the feeling I get from the story? How do I respond to those clues? Why does the author want me to feel this way?

Thinking about synonyms and antonyms for words authors use will help you read more critically. You might ask: What words are **synonyms** or **antonyms** for this word? Why did the author choose this word instead of one of its synonyms? How does knowing its antonym help me understand the sentence?

In this unit, recognizing **mood** and evaluating **synonyms and antonyms** will help you become an active reader.

Autobiographical Fiction: The Writer's Voice

People from all cultures write about their experiences. In autobiographical fiction, an author bases story events on his or her own life. Many of the events may have happened to the author but the dialogue may be invented. The details and sequence of events are often changed. Reading autobiographical fiction about people from cultures other than our own gives us a close-up view of how other people live, think, and feel.

Responding to Autobiographical Fiction

Compare your own feelings, attitudes, and experiences with those in the story. Jot down your responses as you read the excerpt from *Lost Names* and the story "The Circuit." Use your notes to discuss the stories with classmates.

Mood

| *Lesson 1* | **Introducing** page 2 | **Practicing** page 3 | **Applying** page 4 | **Reviewing** page 16 | **Testing** page 17 |

Introducing Strategies

Authors use details so that their stories affect the reader a certain way. The feeling that story details create is called **mood.** The mood can be joyful, sad, frightening, or mysterious. Sometimes the mood stays the same throughout a story. Other times, it shifts as events change in the plot. Good readers respond to stories by noticing how the details make them feel. Then they think about the author's purpose for wanting them to feel this way.

The diagram below shows the process good readers use to respond to mood and to identify the author's purpose.

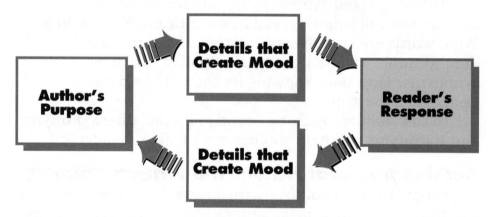

Reading the Novel Excerpt

Read the excerpt from the novel *Lost Names* **on pages 8-10 and the sidenotes on pages 8-9. These notes show how one good reader responded to the mood of the story. After reading, answer the questions below.**

1. The reader thinks the mood near the beginning of the passage is eerie. Which words make the reader feel this way?

_____

_____

2. As the family approaches the other side of the river, the mood changes. What does the reader notice about the changes?

_____

_____

Practicing **Mood**

A. The incomplete statements below are based on the excerpt from *Lost Names*. Circle the letter in front of the word or words that best completes each statement. Then, on the lines provided, give some details from the passage to support your choice.

1. The general mood at the beginning of the excerpt from *Lost Names* can be described as

a. happy.   c. frightened and anxious.

b. exhilarated.   d. confident.

_____

_____

2. The mood throughout the excerpt shifts between

a. peace and grief.   c. fear and hope.

b. excitement and despair.   d. sadness and happiness.

_____

_____

3. The following passage: "After this," she thinks, "I can go with my family anywhere, anytime, to the end of the earth. . . ." at the end of the selection signals a mood that can be described as

a. frightened and anxious.   c. serious and sad.

b. hopeful and proud.   d. a and c above.

_____

_____

B. Describe an important life event. In your description, use details that convey to the reader your feelings about the event.

_____

_____

_____

_____

_____

_____

_____

_____

Applying Mood

A. Read the passage below. As you read, think about the mood that the details create. Then complete the items that follow.

I woke with a start—I should never have fallen asleep out by myself on the boat! I sat up quickly and looked around. The weather had changed. Dark clouds had moved in, and I could see a storm coming in from the sea. Cold gusts of wind flapped the sail. Worst of all, the coastline was fogged in. I checked my watch quickly. It was 5:30. Only about an hour of daylight left. I tried to see the marina. It was hidden in the fog, but I could see the breakwater to its south, so I knew which way to sail. I'd probably be able to see the marina once I got closer. I shivered and struggled into my windbreaker, then started hauling up the anchor. I had to make it back before the storm hit!

1. List some words that describe the mood of the passage.

_____

_____

_____

_____

2. Which details in the passage did the writer use to create the mood?

_____

_____

_____

_____

3. What do you think the writer's purpose is? How does the mood help you understand that purpose?

_____

_____

_____

_____

_____

To review
⬇
page
16

Synonyms and Antonyms

Lesson 2	**Introducing** *page 5*	**Practicing** *page 6*	**Applying** *page 7*	**Reviewing** *page 18*	**Testing** *page 19*

Introducing Strategies

Authors choose their words carefully when they write. Sometimes they choose words that have **synonyms,** or other words that mean the same thing. They may also use words that have **antonyms,** or words that mean the opposite and could change the meaning of a sentence. Like authors, good readers know that thinking about synonyms and antonyms can build their vocabularies for better reading and writing.

The chart below shows how readers can think about synonyms and antonyms while reading.

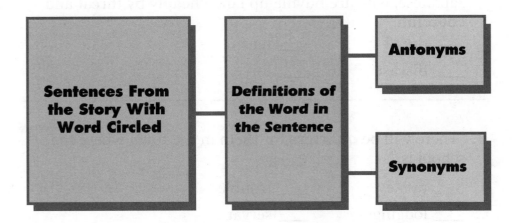

Sentences From the Story With Word Circled — **Definitions of the Word in the Sentence** — **Antonyms** / **Synonyms**

Reading the Novel Excerpt

Read the excerpt from *Lost Names* and circle words for which you can think of synonyms and antonyms. Then answer the questions below, based on the line "Then she is suddenly seized with a violent fear of the strange alien land waiting for her."

1. List a synonym and an antonym for the word *alien*. Use a dictionary or a thesaurus to help you if you wish.

_____

2. How does knowing a synonym and an antonym for *alien* help give you a better picture of the narrator's feelings?

_____

_____

Practicing **Synonyms and Antonyms**

A. Read each of the following quotations from *Lost Names*. **Write a check before the word that is the best synonym for the word in dark type. Then, on the line provided, rewrite the sentence using the synonym you chose.**

1. "People without a country"—my mother thinks—"people **ousted** and uprooted from their homeland."

   ____ annoyed   ____ removed

   ____ led   ____ surprised

   _____

2. ". . . forced out of their land and their homes by the Japanese, who are buying up land cheaply by threat and **coercion**."

   ____ dread   ____ harm

   ____ disease   ____ force

   _____

3. "There will be **quarters** for them in the town where the school is."

   ____ money   ____ trouble

   ____ lodgings   ____ servants

   _____

B. Choose one of the sentences above. Tell why you think the author chose the original word rather than the synonym you used to rewrite the sentence. You may wish to use a dictionary or thesaurus to write your response.

_____

_____

_____

_____

_____

_____

_____

_____

Applying **Synonyms and Antonyms**

Read each sentence. Write a synonym and an antonym for the word in dark type. You may want to use a dictionary or a thesaurus to help you. Then, using the antonym, tell how changing the word changed the meaning of the sentence.

1. We spent days studying a map of the submarine before **embarking** on the tour.

    a. Synonym: _____   b. Antonym: _____

_____

_____

_____

_____

2. Before our submarine tour began, a nearby ship sounded its horn with an **earsplitting** blast.

    a. Synonym: _____   b. Antonym: _____

_____

_____

_____

_____

3. It's hard to believe that a submarine can travel to such underwater **depths.**

    a. Synonym: _____   b. Antonym: _____

_____

_____

_____

_____

4. Compared to the submarine, where I felt so cramped, my small apartment suddenly seemed **huge.**

    a. Synonym: _____   b. Antonym: _____

_____

_____

_____

_____

To review

↓

page 18

In *Lost Names* Richard Kim writes of his childhood in Korea under the occupation of the Japanese. The title comes from the fact that the Japanese forced the Koreans to give up their own names and take Japanese names. This excerpt tells of the escape by night of his family across the frozen Tuman River. It is told from his mother's point of view, as he is an infant in his father's arms at the time the story takes place.

Lost Names

The notes in the margin on pages 8 and 9 show how one reader identified and responded to details that create mood in the story.

by Richard Kim

. . . My father stretches out his hand, which my mother takes as she steps onto the ice. It is the first time they have touched hands since they left home, my grandparents' house. "Do you feel all right?" asks my father. She nods.

. . . They both watch the people helping a young girl up. They look toward the south side of the river, the Korean side, but they can't see anything. With all the snow under the starry sky, the air is strangely white.

The mood is eerie. Richard Kim wants us to feel the strangeness of this procession in white darkness. He says it was "strangely white." People moved "like ghosts."

▶ People move on like ghosts, silently, except for their feet crunching on the ice. "People without a country"—my mother thinks—"people ousted and uprooted from their homeland. Forced out of their land and their homes by the Japanese, who are buying up land cheaply by threat and coercion. Displaced peasants driven out of their ancestral land to find new roots in an alien land." What fate is waiting for these people across the river? What destiny will unfold for her and her family across the

Also I feel the sadness of people who are forced to leave their homeland.

▶ river? She gazes at her husband's back. She can't see the baby. She slips on a large chunk of ice and almost falls. In that second, she lost sight of him and the baby and now she wants desperately to be at their side. She wants to touch him and the baby. She hurries over to them.

My father turns around. "Be careful," he whispers. "Here hold onto my hand." She is out of breath and clings to his outstretched hand. She opens the blanket a little to look at me. "He is all right. Asleep," says my father. "Poor

The mood here is tense. The mother is clearly afraid. One way I can tell is that she needs to touch her husband and child.

▶ thing," she says. "Come," he says, "it won't be long." They are halfway across the river.

Later, the old man ahead of them turns around and says, "You have to be careful now. The ice gets thin around here, and there are holes here and there. Last time I came by, I saw some Chinese fishing through holes." The old man squats down and unwraps a bundle he has been carrying on his back. He takes out a kerosene lantern and tries to light it. The wind blows out his match. The old woman tries to help him by crouching next to him and holding her skirt around the lantern, which the old man lights. "You people stay close behind us. Don't worry. . . ."

"We are almost there," he says. "Almost there now." Almost there. Across the river. She looks toward the bank. There are people standing on the bank. She can see them dimly against the light from the huts. Almost there. Then, it strikes her that there hasn't been anyone going the other way across the river, toward the Korean side. She can hear voices coming from the bank. The sky is clear, and the stars in the northern plains seem larger and brighter than those in other directions. The snow all around her seems so white and almost shining. Her feet are cold and ache, but the crossing is almost over, and she is thinking only that, across the river, someone is waiting for them, someone from the missionary school. She hopes he has brought a buggy with two horses, which, she has heard, people ride in in Manchuria, "Taking a buggy ride in the snow would be nice," she thinks, "just as they do in Russia," or so she has read. Almost there. There will be quarters for them in the town where the school is. Two rooms and a kitchen. Her husband will be a teacher; students will visit them, and, of course, so will his fellow teachers and the missionary people. She, too, will be teaching, at the school's kindergarten. Twenty-five children—so they have written her. Mostly Korean children, but some Chinese and American and Canadian children, too. Almost there, across the river. "Oh—the suitcases," she thinks, "I hope the boy and the train conductor make sure the suitcases were left with the Chinese station master. Some wool in one of the suitcases. I will knit a wool sweater for him so he can wear it under his coat when he goes to school to teach, and the baby could use another wool jacket, and maybe another wool cap. Almost there now." "Is the baby still sleeping?" she asks her husband. "Yes," he says. "Just a little more and we'll be there."

The old man's lantern, the lights along the bank like haloes, and the voices calling to them. Almost there now. Then, she is suddenly seized with a violent fear of that strange alien land waiting for her. All those Chinese people there. "The town is almost a Korean town, really,"

◀ Even though these people are being kind to them, I'm getting more and more scared. It would be awful to fall through the ice.

◀ The mood shifts with the clear sky and bright stars. Freezing as she is, the mother is excited and pleased that someone will be meeting them. I think Richard Kim wants us to feel hopeful.

As you read the rest of the story, think about how the story details make you feel. Then write your own sidenotes about the mood of the story.

her husband has said to her, "and the school, of course, is for Korean students. It really is like any other Korean town, except that there are lots of Chinese people around you." "A Korean ghetto, that's what it is," she thinks. She has heard from her father that, in many places in Europe, the Jewish people lived together among foreigners who did not welcome them, and the places where they lived were called the ghettos. "Like our parish," he said: "We Christians in this country live close to each other around our churches, and that is not much different from the Jewish people living in their ghettos." "Will those Chinese people be friendly?" she wants to ask her husband, but it is not the time to ask a question like that. Almost there. And, suddenly, she again thinks of holes and thin ice and big cracks in the ice. Thin ice, holes, cracks. . . . The bank looms ahead of them, and it is as if, with one big leap over the ice, they can get onto it. But, now that they are so close to the other side of the river, she feels as if she is losing all her will and strength. "We have made it across," she says to herself. And again—holes, cracks, and thin ice frighten her. Thin ice especially. For one moment, she has a blinding vision of crashing through thin ice and being sucked into the cold water and pushed down under the ice . . . one of her hands is clinging to the edge of the ice, but her body is being pulled down and down . . . and the water freezes her instantly and she can't even scream for help but, then, her husband pulls her up out of the water onto the ice and she gets up . . . and asks, "Is the baby still asleep?"

He says, "Yes."

She says to him, squeezing his hand, "We've made it, haven't we?"

"We've made it across," he says, looking straight ahead.

"Good thing the baby slept through."

He turns to her. "Actually, he's been wide awake. All the way."

She smiles. "What a good little boy he is," she says. She is not thinking of the thin ice, holes, and big cracks in the ice any longer. After this, she thinks, I can go with my family anywhere, anytime, to the end of the earth. . . .

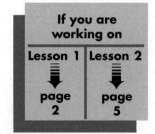

If you are working on

| Lesson 1 | Lesson 2 |
| page 2 | page 5 |

Francisco Jiménez (1943-) has said about this story: "[It] is an autobiographical story based on my childhood experiences." Jiménez was born in Mexico, but his family moved to Santa Maria, California, when he was three years old. There, the family lived as migrant workers. This story shares some of the details of such a life.

The Circuit

by Francisco Jiménez

Write your own sidenotes as you read. Identify the details that create a mood or feeling as you read. Note why you think the author wanted you to feel this way.

It was that time of year again. Ito, the strawberry sharecropper, did not smile. It was natural. The peak of the strawberry season was over and the last few days the workers, most of them *braceros,* were not picking as many boxes as they had during the months of June and July.

As the last days of August disappeared, so did the number of *braceros.* Sunday, only one—the best picker—came to work. I liked him. Sometimes we talked during our half-hour lunch break. That is how I found out he was from Jalisco, the same state in Mexico my family was from. That Sunday was the last time I saw him.

When the sun had tired and sunk behind the mountains, Ito signaled us that it was time to go home. *"Ya esora,"* he yelled in his broken Spanish. Those were the words I waited for twelve hours a day, every day, seven days a week, week after week. And the thought of not hearing them again saddened me.

As we drove home Papá did not say a word. With both hands on the wheel, he stared at the dirt road. My older brother, Roberto, was also silent. He leaned his head back and closed his eyes. Once in a while he cleared from his throat the dust that blew in from outside.

Yes, it was that time of year. When I opened the front door to the shack, I stopped. Everything we owned was neatly packed in cardboard boxes. Suddenly I felt even more the weight of hours, days, weeks, and months of work. I sat down on a box. The thought of having to move to Fresno and knowing what was in store for me there brought tears to my eyes. . . .

Everything was packed except Mamá's pot. It was an old large galvanized pot she had picked up at an army surplus store in Santa María the year I was born. The pot had many dents and nicks, and the more dents and nicks it acquired the more Mamá liked it. *"Mi olla,"* she used to say proudly.

I held the front door open as Mamá carefully carried out her pot by both handles, making sure not to spill the cooked beans. When she got to the car, Papá reached out to help her with it. Roberto opened the rear car door and Papá gently placed it on the floor behind the front seat. All of us then climbed in. Papá sighed, wiped the sweat off his forehead with his sleeve, and said wearily: *"Es todo."*

As we drove away, I felt a lump in my throat. I turned around and looked at our little shack for the last time.

At sunset we drove into a labor camp near Fresno. Since Papá did not speak English, Mamá asked the camp foreman if he needed any more workers. "We don't need no more," said the foreman, scratching his head. "Check with Sullivan down the road. Can't miss him. He lives in a big white house with a fence around it."

When we got there, Mamá walked up to the house. She went through a white gate, past a row of rose bushes, up the stairs to the front door. She rang the doorbell. The porch light went on and a tall husky man came out. They exchanged a few words. After the man went in, Mamá clasped her hands and hurried back to the car. "We have work! Mr. Sullivan said we can stay there the whole season," she said, gasping and pointing to an old garage near the stables.

The garage was worn out by the years. It had no windows. The walls, eaten by termites, strained to support the roof full of holes. The dirt floor, populated by earth worms, looked like a gray road map.

That night, by the light of a kerosene lamp, we unpacked and cleaned our new home. Roberto swept away the loose dirt, leaving the hard ground. Papá plugged the holes in the walls with old newspapers and tin can tops. Mamá fed my little brothers and sisters. Papá and Roberto then brought in the mattress and placed it on the far corner of the garage. "Mamá, you and the little ones sleep on the mattress. Roberto, Panchito, and I will sleep outside under the trees," Papá said.

Early next morning Mr. Sullivan showed us where his crop was, and after breakfast, Papá, Roberto, and I headed for the vineyard to pick. . . .

Suddenly I noticed Papá's face turn pale as he looked down the road. "Here comes the school bus," he whispered loudly in alarm. Instinctively, Roberto and I ran and hid in the vineyards. We did not want to get in trouble for not going to school. The neatly dressed boys about my age got off. They carried books under their arms. After they crossed the street, the bus drove away. Roberto and I came out from hiding and joined Papá. *"Tienen que tener cuidado,"* he warned us.

After lunch we went back to work. The sun kept beating down. The buzzing insects, the wet sweat, and the hot dry dust made the afternoon seem to last forever. Finally the mountains around the valley reached out and swallowed the sun. Within an hour it was too dark to continue picking. The vines blanketed the grapes, making it difficult to see the bunches. *"Vámonos,"* said Papá, signaling to us that it was time to quit work. Papá then took out a pencil and began to figure out how much we had earned our first day. He wrote down numbers, crossed some out, wrote down some more. *"Quince,"* he murmured.

When we arrived home, we took a cold shower underneath a waterhose. We then sat down to eat dinner around some wooden crates that served as a table. Mamá had cooked a special meal for us. We had rice and tortillas with *"carne con chile,"* my favorite dish.

The next morning I could hardly move. My body ached all over. I felt little control over my arms and legs. This feeling went on every morning for days until my muscles finally got used to the work.

It was Monday, the first week of November. The grape season was over and I could now go to school. I woke up early that morning and lay in bed, looking at the stars and savoring the thought of not going to work and of starting sixth grade for the first time that year. Since I could not sleep, I decided to get up and join Papá and Roberto at breakfast. I sat at the table across from Roberto, but I kept my head down. I did not want to look up and face him. I knew he was sad. He was not going to school today. He was not going tomorrow, or next week, or next month. He would not go until the cotton season was over, and that was sometime in February. I rubbed my hands together and watched the dry, acid-stained skin fall to the floor in little rolls.

When Papá and Roberto left for work, I felt relief. I walked to the top of a small grade next to the shack and watched the "Carcanchita" disappear in the distance in a cloud of dust.

Two hours later, around eight o'clock, I stood by the side of the road waiting for school bus number twenty. When it arrived, I climbed in. Everyone was busy either talking or yelling. I sat in an empty seat in the back.

When the bus stopped in front of the school, I felt very nervous. I looked out the bus window and saw boys and girls carrying books under their arms. I put my hands in my pants pockets and walked to the principal's office. When I entered, I heard a woman's voice say: "May I help you?" I was startled. I had not heard English for months. For a few seconds I remained speechless. I looked at the lady who waited for an answer. My first instinct was to answer her in Spanish, but I held back. Finally, after struggling for English words, I managed to tell her that I wanted to enroll in the sixth grade. After answering many questions, I was led to the classroom.

Mr. Lema, the sixth grade teacher, greeted me and assigned me a desk. He then introduced me to the class. I was so nervous and scared at that moment when everyone's eyes were on me that I wished I were with Papá and Roberto picking cotton. After taking roll, Mr. Lema gave the class the assignment for the first hour. "The first thing we have to do this morning is finish reading the story we began yesterday," he said enthusiastically. He walked up to me, handed me an English book, and asked me to read. "We are on page 125," he said politely. When I heard this, I felt my blood rush to my head; I felt dizzy. "Would you like to read?" he asked hesitantly. I opened the book to page 125. My mouth was dry. My eyes began to water. I could not begin. "You can read later," Mr. Lema said understandingly.

For the rest of the reading period I kept getting angrier and angrier with myself. I should have read, I thought to myself.

During recess I went into the restroom and opened my English book to page 125. I began to read in a low voice, pretending I was in class. There were many words I did not know. I closed the book and headed back to the classroom.

Mr. Lema was sitting at his desk correcting papers. When I entered, he looked up at me and smiled. I felt better. I walked up to him and asked if he could help me with the new words. "Gladly," he said.

The rest of the month I spent my lunch hours working on English with Mr. Lema, my best friend at school.

One Friday during lunch hour Mr. Lema asked me to take a walk with him to the music room. "Do you like music?" he asked me as we entered the building.

"Yes, I like *corridos*," I answered. He then picked up a trumpet, blew on it and handed it to me. The sound gave me goose bumps. I knew that sound. I had heard it in many corridos. "How would you like to learn how to play it?" he asked. He must have read my face because before I could answer, he added: "I'll teach you how to play it during our lunch hours."

That day I could hardly wait to get home to tell Papá and Mamá the great news. As I got off the bus, my little brothers and sisters ran up to meet me. They were yelling and screaming. I thought they were happy to see me, but when I opened the door to our shack, I saw that everything we owned was neatly packed in cardboard boxes.

If you are working on

Lesson 1 — page 16

Lesson 2 — page 18

Reviewing Mood

A. Read the story "The Circuit" on pages 11-15. As you read, write some notes in the margins about the mood of the story and details that create the mood. Think about why the author may have wanted the reader to feel this way. Use the diagram below to record some of your responses.

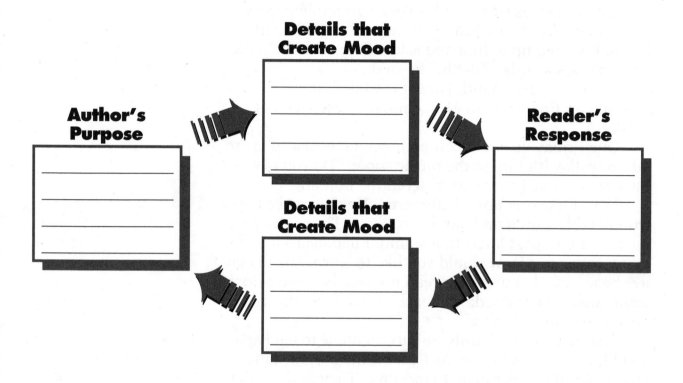

Details that Create Mood

Author's Purpose

Details that Create Mood

Reader's Response

B. Describe the mood of the story "The Circuit." Does the mood change in any part of the story or does it remain the same throughout? Give examples from the diagram to support your response.

_____

_____

_____

_____

_____

_____

_____

_____

Testing Mood

A. Read the statements below about "The Circuit." Fill in the circle next to the words that best complete each statement. On the lines provided, give some details from the story that support your response.

1. The mood of the first five paragraphs in the story "The Circuit" can be described as
  ○ happy and cheerful.
  ○ sad and regretful.
  ○ calm and peaceful.
  ○ filled with suspense.

_____

_____

2. The author's purpose in the story "The Circuit" can best be summarized as
  ○ to give a realistic view of the migrant worker's hard and unsettling life.
  ○ to express the importance of the migrant worker's family life.
  ○ to show that children of migrant workers must change schools often.
  ○ to point out that people should do more to help the migrant workers.

_____

_____

B. Imagine you are the child in "The Circuit." Write a paragraph telling how you felt at the end of the story. Include details in your writing that reflect your feelings and establish the mood.

_____

_____

_____

_____

_____

_____

To begin
Lesson 2

↓

page
5

Reviewing **Synonyms and Antonyms**

A. Reread the story "The Circuit" on pages 11-15. As you read, circle words for which you can think of synonyms and antonyms. Then use one of the words you circled to complete the chart below.

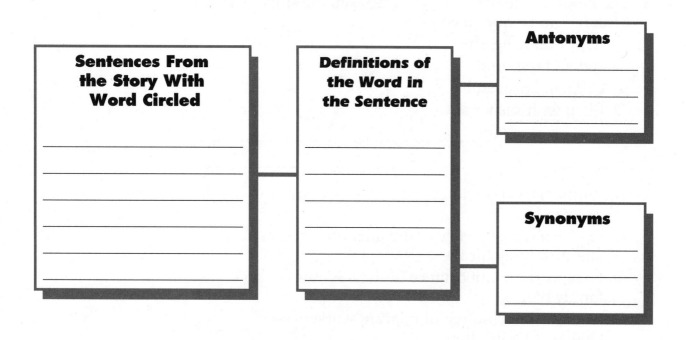

Sentences From the Story With Word Circled

Definitions of the Word in the Sentence

Antonyms

Synonyms

B. Write a paragraph about the importance of migrant farm workers in the United States today. Use your own ideas. Look up additional information, as needed, in an encyclopedia or other reference. Use at least two synonyms or two antonyms in your writing.

Testing Synonyms and Antonyms

A. Read the passage below. Read it a second time and fill each blank with a word from the pairs of synonyms and antonyms listed in the right-hand margin. Choose the word that makes the most sense in the story.

Being the elder son in a three-generation family restaurant has its _____ moments—especially since, at age 17,

(1)

I am already responsible for making out the _____

(2)

payroll. And while it's true that I'm a _____ math

(3)

student, keeping the books for a staff of 30 people is a big job

and _____ to the success of Mario's Café.

(4)

I have two younger sisters and a younger brother, all of

whom also work _____ at Mario's after school and

(5)

on weekends. My parents have little time for _____

(6)

but they don't seem to mind. So, what's the secret to the

_____ of Mario's Café? A family that likes to work

(7)

_____ and—oh, yes—the best linguine in town!

(8)

1. strenuous
   easy
2. yearly
   weekly
3. weak
   strong
4. critical
   unimportant
5. eagerly
   hesitantly
6. vacation
   work
7. failure
   success
8. together
   alone

B. Think about a movie you watched recently. List two negative words and two positive words that describe the movie. Then list two synonyms and two antonyms for each word on your list. Write a paragraph describing how they are different from the words you chose originally.

_____

_____

_____

_____

_____

_____

_____

_____

Unit TWO

BECOMING AN ACTIVE READER

Good readers are active readers. When reading **autobiographical fiction** they imagine that they are part of the story. They visualize the settings and characters. Good readers make themselves part of the story by bringing their own experiences to it.

Using Skills and Strategies

Identifying the story's **point of view** will help you become involved in your reading. You might ask: Whose story is this? Who is telling the story? How does that person think and feel? In what ways am I like him or her?

To become actively involved in stories you may also need to **draw conclusions**, or read between the lines. To draw conclusions, you might ask: What has the writer described here in the story? What do I know about a similar situation?

In this unit, the skills of identifying **point of view** and **drawing conclusions** will help you read the stories actively.

Reading Autobiographical Fiction

Some authors write fiction that is based on events in their own lives. By reading their stories, we get a glimpse into their experiences, feelings, and attitudes. Even when the stories tell about events that we have never experienced, we can find something that is very familiar—feelings and emotions that are the same for all people.

Responding to Autobiographical Fiction

Good readers usually respond to stories by identifying with the characters. As you read the two selections in this unit, "The All-American Girl" and the excerpt from "Where the Red Fern Grows," jot down your thoughts and feelings. Use these sidenotes when you discuss the stories with your classmates.

Point of View

| Lesson 3 | Introducing page 21 | Practicing page 22 | Applying page 23 | Reviewing page 33 | Testing page 34 |

Introducing Strategies

Good readers know that the **point of view,** or angle, from which a story is being told can affect how they respond to the characters and events. In first-person stories, narrators are main characters who use the words *I, me,* or *we* and focus on their own thoughts and feelings. In third-person stories, narrators describe events and characters from outside the story and use the words *he, she,* or *they.* The words *I* or *me* appear in a third-person story in passages that contain dialogue.

The chart below shows how readers identify the point of view and then note their responses.

Question	Look Back	Respond
Who is the narrator? Which words tell the reader?	What are some examples that illustrate the point of view?	How does the point of view affect my response?

Reading the Short Story

Read "The All-American Girl" on pages 27-29 and the sidenotes on pages 27-28. The notes show how one good reader responded to the story's point of view. Then answer the questions below.

1. The reader suggests that the story is told from Hajime's brother's point of view. Is this a first-person or a third-person point of view?

_____

_____

2. What does the reader think about the narrator's involvement with the girl?

_____

_____

Practicing *Point of View*

A. Circle the letter of the choice that best completes each sentence below. Then, on the lines provided, explain why you selected that answer.

1. At the beginning of this story, the narrator
   a. was more interested in the girl than his brother.
   b. coined the phrase the "All-American" girl.
   c. described Hajime's fascination with the girl.
   d. knew exactly how he felt about the girl.

_____

_____

2. If the story had been written from a third-person point of view, the outside narrator may have
   a. revealed more about the girl's feelings.
   b. told more about Hajime's brother.
   c. explained why Hajime called the girl "All-American."
   d. a, b, and c.

_____

_____

3. In this story, both the narrator and Hajime
   a. disagree about whether or not to talk to the girl.
   b. agree not to destroy the image they have of the girl.
   c. engage in a conversation with the girl.
   d. do none of the above.

_____

_____

B. Imagine you are the All-American girl. Describe what has been happening from *your* point of view.

_____

_____

_____

_____

_____

_____

_____

Applying *Point of View*

A. The excerpt below is from *Children of the River* by Linda Crew. It is the story of Sundara Sovann, a teenager who fled war-torn Cambodia and emigrated to the United States. Sundara respects her own culture, yet she yearns to be accepted in her Oregon high school.

> . . . *She looked away from him, across the patio, stalling for time. A date. He was actually asking her out on a date. A picture flashed in her mind: Jonathan on the doorstep, like in the TV commercials, Naro and Soka looking him over, making him promise to bring her home on time. . . . No, no, never in a thousand years . . . She turned back to Jonathan.*
>
> *"Thank you, but I cannot. . . . I like to go with you, but— in my country, we don't go out on a date at all. . . . Our parents arrange. . . ."*
>
> *"But that's . . . archaic."*

1. Think about the narrator in this excerpt. Is it someone inside or outside the story? From whose point of view is the story told?

_____

_____

2. At the beginning of the excerpt, the author uses the pronouns *she, he,* and *her.* Toward the end of the excerpt, the author uses the pronouns *I, we, you,* and *our* in the dialogue. Which pronouns gave you a clue to identifying the point of view?

_____

_____

B. Rewrite the excerpt from Jonathan's point of view. Share your first-person narrative with classmates.

_____

_____

_____

_____

_____

_____

To review
↓
page
33

Drawing Conclusions

Lesson 4	Introducing *page 24*	Practicing *page 25*	Applying *page 26*	Reviewing *page 35*	Testing *page 36*

Introducing Strategies

Has anyone ever said to you, "Don't jump to conclusions"? That person is telling you not to make a judgment or form an opinion about something without adequate evidence. Good readers look for evidence, or clues, about characters and events in the stories they read. They relate the evidence to their own experiences in order to draw an informed conclusion.

The diagram below shows how readers use evidence from the story and their own experiences to **draw** logical **conclusions.**

Reading the Short Story

Reread "The All-American Girl" on pages 27-29. Underline places in the story where you drew a logical or an informed conclusion about the characters or events. Then answer the questions below.

1. What is one conclusion that you drew while reading? On what evidence in the story did you base that conclusion?

_____

_____

2. What thoughts and experiences may have helped you draw that conclusion?

_____

_____

Practicing Drawing Conclusions

A. The questions below are based on the short story "The All-American Girl." Circle the letter next to the sentence that you think best answers each question. Then, on the lines provided, support your conclusion with evidence—a detail or clue from the story.

1. Why did the narrator and Hajime keep watching the girl?
   a. She sometimes wore a yellow hat.
   b. They were fascinated by her beauty and frailty.
   c. She was mysterious and they were curious.
   d. both b and c.

   _____

   _____

2. What do you think made the girl happy the first time they saw her smile?
   a. She had the company of a friend.
   b. She liked her daily walk.
   c. She liked the two people on the porch.
   d. None of the above.

   _____

   _____

3. Why did the girl stop coming by?
   a. Her fiance would not let her.
   b. She was busy preparing for her wedding.
   c. She was upset by the people on the porch.
   d. She was embarrassed by the photograph in the newspaper.

   _____

   _____

B. Describe a favorite character from a TV show, a movie or from your reading. Provide details so that readers can draw conclusions about what the character is like and how you feel about him or her.

   _____

   _____

   _____

   _____

Applying *Drawing Conclusions*

Read the paragraphs below. Then answer the questions that follow.

> *The beat of rock music from across the street made Leon rush to the window. He watched for a moment, then he went back to his desk and picked up the pencil. He looked in the open book and began to take notes, but his pencil seemed more interested in mimicking the drum beat from outside.*
>
> *"Back to work," he told himself sternly and scanned a couple of pages. He was interested in soil testing, and the project was due tomorrow. It suddenly seemed so hard to write. Leon shifted in his chair, got up and went to the kitchen for a glass of water. He ignored the window. He wanted to tell them to turn off the music, he wanted to. . . .*

1. What conclusion did you draw about what Leon really wanted to do?

_____

_____

_____

_____

_____

2. Look back at the paragraph for details that helped you draw this conclusion. List the details.

_____

_____

_____

_____

3. List thoughts or experiences of your own that helped you come to this conclusion.

_____

To review
⬇
page 35

_____

_____

_____

_____

The All-American Girl

by Toshio Mori

We call her the All-American Girl, my brother and I. My brother started calling her that one day. We used to sit on the front porch of our house in the city and every once so often she used to walk past our house. We did not know her name. We watched her walk by, looking neither side, just walking in her trim little way. She walked by in a manner as if she was not aware of us, and possibly that was the beginning of the rub.

◄ I can tell by the use of the words *I, my,* and *we* that the narrator is a main character in the story and has a brother, Hajime.

"There's a beauty," Hajime said one day when she passed. "Isn't she a beauty?"

"I don't know. I guess so," I said. It was the first time I had noticed her.

"She is a beauty," he said. "One of those frail beauties who makes history."

After that we could not help but notice her. She was like most Japanese girls, small, not more than five feet high. Unlike the girls of her size who are lively, restless, and energetic, her tininess made her look all the more frail.

◄ The narrator is telling more about Hajime's thoughts than his or her own here. But it's getting me involved in the story.

"Here comes the beauty," Hajime said when she came down the street. "An All-American if there ever was one."

"Do you think so?" I said.

"Don't you think so?" he said.

I did not say anything. I did not know. One moment she looked frail and ordinary. The next moment she looked frail and extraordinary. She continued to pass the house. Each time she passed my brother commented. "She is the All-American Girl." He said it over and over. "Look how she carries herself," he said one day. "I wish I could put her on paper." He was going to an art school to be an artist. But he did not sketch her. We sat and watched her walk down the street.

◄ It seems that the narrator is getting just as involved with the girl as Hajime. But the narrator is somewhat aloof and says "I don't know."

One day she came by the house accompanied by another girl. They walked gaily and we heard her laugh and talk. We saw her face in smiles as she went by. The

◄ I wonder why the narrator isn't revealing much to Hajime about his or her thoughts and feelings.

next day she came by the house again, this time alone. Her face which was laughter and talk and smiles was gone, and we saw her frail face again. Something is going on here, I said to myself, something is happening.

"What are you thinking about?" my brother said laughingly.

"The All-American was here," I said.

"You say it almost naturally," he said and laughed.

After that we both called her All-American. She came by the house almost regularly. We sat on the front porch and watched her go by. We did not speak to her but we knew she was aware of us and she knew we were aware of her. . . .

This is a turning point. Now the narrator is as involved with the girl as Hajime.

Write your own sidenotes as you read the rest of the story. In your notes, comment on how the author's choice of point of view affects how you respond to the story.

One day we sat and waited for her on the porch. She came late in the afternoon. When she came in sight Hajime stopped sketching. When she passed the house he said, "She must come from a well-to-do home. Her clothes are of finest materials."

There was a time when I sat alone on the porch all day. Hajime was unusually late returning from the art class. The day was cloudy. I had been noticing this all afternoon and just as I looked up for the thirteenth or fourteenth time I found myself gazing into the All-American Girl's face and she was smiling. A moment later she was gone. I looked at her till she turned the block and disappeared. Beautiful, beautiful, I thought. When Hajime finally returned from school, I told him how the All-American Girl came into vision and smiled and was gone. My brother laughed.

"You must have been dreaming this afternoon."

"No, no," I said. "She came five-thirty in the afternoon. She was wearing her yellow dress."

Next day Hajime and I were together again on the porch. She came quite early that day and when she saw us, she smiled. We smiled back and the moment was soon over and she was gone. "This is beautiful. Beautiful," Hajime said. "No words, no gestures. Nothing dramatic but all the drama in the world."

"We shall see," I said.

"She's ours. Our All-American Girl," Hajime said.

"Yes," I said, "but she does not know she is an All American to us."

"No," he said.

After that whenever she saw us she smiled. We said hello and greetings became quite the thing. But it never went beyond that.

"Shouldn't we go through with the adventure?"

Hajime said to me. "All this is beautiful, yes. All this beauty is the halfway mark. Shouldn't we go through with this and see the ugly that is human?"

"No, Hajime. This once," I said, "let's sit and watch the beautiful. Let's have something beautiful to cling to without the ugliness."

"All right," he said. "We do not know her and she is beautiful."

"If something should happen now it would be beautiful all around," I said. "Something like life itself or circumstances breaking into our company."

"That would be beautiful," he said.

Something did happen several weeks later.

We sat for days on the front porch without seeing her. Hajime wanted to know why this unusual thing was happening. "She will be coming along," I said. Then one day in the *Mainichi News* we saw her picture and the announcement of her marriage to a promising doctor in Los Angeles. It was the answer to her absence on our street. We learned her name for the first time. "Her name was Ayako Saito. That is our All-American Girl," Hajime said. "We will never see her again unless we are lucky."

"She was beautiful," I said.

We sat on the front steps and watched the sun go down beyond the rooftops and the trees.

If you are working on

Lesson 3	Lesson 4
⬇	⬇
page 21	page 24

from *Where the Red Fern Grows*

by Wilson Rawls

. . . Grandpa shouted, "Hold up a minute. I'm just about all in."

We stopped.

"Do you think that hound knows what she's doing?" the judge asked. "Maybe we're just running around in circles."

Looking at me, Papa said, "I hope she does. Some of these canebrakes cover miles. If we get lost in here, we'll be in bad shape."

Grandpa said, "I think we've gone too far. The last time I heard Old Dan, he sounded quite close."

"That was because the wind carried the sound," I said.

The judge spoke up, "Fellows, no dog is worth the lives of three men. Now let's do the smart thing and get out of here while we can. Our clothes are wet. If we keep on wandering around in this jungle, we'll freeze to death. It doesn't look like this blizzard is ever going to let up."

I could hear the roar of the blizzard back in the thick timber of the bottoms. Two large limbs being rubbed together by the strong wind made a grinding creaking sound. The tall slender cane around us rattled and swayed.

I could feel the silence closing in. I knew the judge's cold logic had had its effect on my father and grandfather. The men had given up. There was no hope left for me.

Kneeling down, I put my arms around Little Ann. I felt the warm heat from her moist tongue caressing my ear. Closing my eyes, I said, "Please, Dan, bawl one more time, just one more time."

I waited for my plea to be answered.

With its loud roaring, the north wind seemed to be laughing at us. All around, tall stalks of cane were weaving and dancing to the rattling rhythm of their knife-edged blades.

My father tried to talk above the wind, but his words were lost in the storm. Just before another blast, clear as a foghorn on a stormy sea, Old Dan's voice rang loud and clear. It seemed louder than the roar of the wind or the skeleton-like rustling of the tall swaying cane.

I jumped to my feet. My heart did a complete flip-flop. The knot in my throat felt as big as an apple. I tried to whoop, but it was no use. Little Ann bawled and tugged on the rope.

There was no mistaking the direction. We knew that Little Ann had been right all along. Straight as an arrow, she had led us to him.

Old Dan was treed down in a deep gully. I slid off the bank and ran to him. His back was covered with a layer of frozen sleet. His frost-covered whiskers stood out straight as porcupine quills.

I worked the wedges of ice from between his toes, and scraped the sleet from his body with my hands. Little Ann came over and tried to wash his face. He didn't like it. Jerking loose from me, he ran over to the tree, reared up on it, and started bawling.

Hearing shouting from the bank above me, I looked up. I could dimly see Papa and the judge through the driving sleet. At first I thought they were shouting to me, but on peering closer I could see that they had their backs to me. Catching hold of some long stalks of cane that were hanging down from the steep bank, I pulled myself up.

Papa shouted in my ear, "Something has happened to your grandfather."

Turning to the judge, he said, "He was behind you. When was the last time you saw him?"

"I don't know for sure," the judge said. "I guess it was back there when we heard the hound bawl."

"Didn't you hear anything?" Papa asked.

"Hear anything?" the judge exclaimed. "How could I hear anything in all that noise? I thought he was behind me all the time, and didn't miss him until we got here."

I couldn't hold back the tears. My grandfather was lost and wandering in that white jungle of cane. Screaming for him, I started back.

Papa caught me. He shouted, "Don't do that."

I tried to tear away from him but his grip on my arm was firm.

"Shoot the gun," the judge said.

Papa shot time after time. It was useless. We got no answer.

from *Where the Red Fern Grows* ■ 31

Little Ann came up out of the washout. She stood and stared at me. Turning, she disappeared quickly in the thick cane. Minutes later we heard her. It was a long, mournful cry.

The only times I had ever heard my little dog bawl like that were when she was baying at a bright Ozark moon, or when someone played a French harp or a fiddle close to her ear. She didn't stop until we reached her.

Grandpa lay as he had fallen, face down in the icy sleet. His right foot was wedged in the fork of a broken box elder limb. When the ankle had twisted, the searing pain must have made him unconscious.

Papa worked Grandpa's foot free and turned him over. I sat down and placed his head in my lap. While Papa and the judge massaged his arms and legs, I wiped the frozen sleet from his eyes and face.

Burying my face in the iron-gray hair, I cried and begged God not to let my grandfather die.

"I think he's gone," the judge said.

"I don't think so," Papa said. "He took a bad fall when that limb tripped him, but he hasn't been lying here long enough to be frozen. I think he's just unconscious."

Papa lifted him to a sitting position and told the judge to start slapping his face. Grandpa moaned and moved his head.

"He's coming around," Papa said.

I asked Papa if we could get him back to the gully where Old Dan was. I had noticed there was very little wind there and we could build a fire.

"That's the very place," he said. "We'll build a good fire and one of us can go for help."

Papa and the judge made a seat by catching each other's wrists. They eased Grandpa between them.

By the time we reached the washout, Grandpa was fully conscious again, and was mumbling and grumbling.

He couldn't see why they had to carry him like a baby. . . .

If you are working on

Lesson 3	Lesson 4
⬇	⬇
page 33	page 35

Reviewing *Point of View*

A. Read the excerpt from *Where the Red Fern Grows* on pages 30-32. As you read, identify examples of the point of view and how they affect your responses to the story. Then use your notes to fill in the diagram below.

Question ➔	**Look Back** ➔	**Respond**
Who is the narrator? _____ _____ _____	What are some examples that illustrate the point of view? _____ _____ _____ _____	How does the point of view affect my response? _____ _____ _____ _____
Which words tell me? _____ _____ _____	_____ _____ _____	_____ _____ _____

B. Identify one part of the story where you think the author's choice of point of view is particularly effective. Explain why you made this choice.

_____

_____

_____

_____

_____

_____

_____

_____

_____

_____

Testing Point of View

A. The questions below are based on the novel excerpt from *Where the Red Fern Grows*. Fill in the oval next to each true statement. Then, on the lines provided, explain why you chose the statement.

1. ○ The words, *"Papa shouted in my ear, 'Something has happened to your grandfather,'"* tell readers that Papa is the narrator.

    ○ The words *"Papa shouted in my ear, 'Something has happened to your grandfather,'"* tell readers that the narrator is one of the story characters.

    _____

    _____

2. ○ The story is written from the first-person point of view.

    ○ The story is written from the third-person point of view.

    _____

    _____

3. ○ In the story, the narrator describes the action and also tells readers about his own thoughts and feelings.

    ○ In the story, the narrator is distant, describing only the events and telling no one's feelings.

    _____

    _____

B. How do you think Billy's grandfather felt as he regained consciousness? Write about this event from Billy's grandfather's point of view.

_____

_____

_____

_____

_____

_____

_____

To begin
Lesson 4

↓

page
24

Reviewing *Drawing Conclusions*

A. Reread the excerpt from *Where the Red Fern Grows* on pages 30-32. As you read, underline places in the story where you drew some logical conclusions. When you are finished, select the most important conclusion you noted to complete the diagram below.

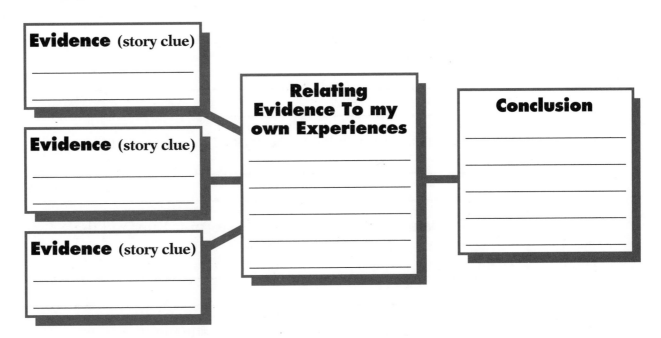

Evidence (story clue)

_____
_____

Evidence (story clue)

_____
_____

Evidence (story clue)

_____
_____

Relating Evidence To my own Experiences

_____
_____
_____
_____

Conclusion

_____
_____
_____
_____
_____

B. Describe a mysterious incident you heard about or saw in a movie or on TV. In your description, provide evidence—clues or details—so that your readers can draw some reasonable conclusions.

_____
_____
_____
_____
_____
_____
_____
_____
_____
_____
_____

Testing Drawing Conclusions

A. Each statement below is a conclusion based on the excerpt from *Where the Red Fern Grows*. Fill in the oval next to each conclusion that makes sense. On the lines provided, explain why you did or did not think the statement was a logical conclusion. Look for evidence in the story to support your response.

1. ○ Billy had more faith in the dogs than either his papa or the judge.

_____

_____

2. ○ Little Ann is a less experienced dog than Dan.

_____

_____

3. ○ Dan would have died in the storm if Billy and the others hadn't found him.

_____

_____

4. ○ Dan had a raccoon cornered in the big tree.

_____

_____

5. ○ The judge is a person who gives up easily.

_____

_____

B. Would it be logical to conclude from this excerpt that Little Ann was a better tracking and hunting hound than Billy's favorite, Old Dan? On the lines below, write a paragraph that states your conclusion. Include some details from the story that support your conclusion.

_____

_____

_____

_____

_____

Unit THREE

BECOMING AN ACTIVE READER

Good readers are strategic readers. When they read **persuasive letters** they evaluate each statement carefully. They weigh these statements against their own needs, values, and interests. Then they decide if the writer has convinced them to take an action.

Using Skills and Strategies

Noting persuasive techniques as you **read persuasive letters** will help you decide if you want to do what a letter suggests. Questions that you might ask include: Why is the writer sending the letter? What action does the writer want me to take? Has the writer convinced me to take that action? Why or why not?

Noting the **origin of words** in persuasive letters can help you read strategically. As you come across a word, you might ask: Do I recognize part of the word? Do I know the meaning of a word that might have a similar root? Does its origin provide a clue to why the writer used it?

In this unit, the skills of **reading persuasive letters** and noting **word origins** will help you become a strategic reader.

Persuasive Letters: The Writer's Voice

One way organizations get their messages across is to write persuasive letters. They try to convince an audience to take some action. Writing persuasive letters and sending them to a select audience is an important way for diverse groups in our culture to communicate their ideas and goals.

Responding to Persuasive Letters

Writing sidenotes will help you analyze the persuasive letters from the INMED Program and Quercus State College in this unit. Refer to your notes when you discuss the letters with your classmates.

Reading Persuasive Letters

Lesson 5	Introducing *page 38*	Practicing *page 39*	Applying *page 40*	Reviewing *page 48*	Testing *page 49*

Introducing Strategies

Persuasive letters are aimed at a specific audience. People who write persuasive letters want to convince readers in that audience to behave or think a certain way. To do this, writers use facts or statistics that appeal to reason. They also appeal to the readers' emotions by making statements that focus on strong feelings—for example: *Are you out on a limb? We can help!* Good readers evaluate persuasive writing before changing their thinking or behavior. As you **read persuasive letters,** ask yourself: Is the writer effective in convincing me to take an action? How has the letter changed my thinking?

The chart below shows you how to analyze persuasive letters by looking for details that appeal to reason and details that appeal to emotions.

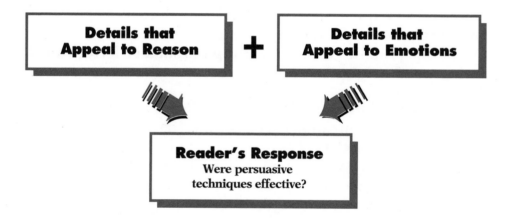

Reading the Persuasive Letter

Read the "Indians Into Medicine" letter on pages 44-45 and read the sidenotes on page 44. The sidenotes show how one good reader analyzed details in the letter that appeal to reason and details that appeal to emotion.

1. List some details from the letter that appeal to the reader's reason.

_____

2. What details appeal to the reader's emotions?

_____

Practicing **Reading Persuasive Letters**

A. Each incomplete statement below is based on the "Indians Into Medicine" letter on pages 44-45. Circle the letter before the word or words that best complete each statement. Then explain your choices on the lines provided.

1. The letter is aimed at
   a. health professionals.
   b. Native American students in grades 7-12.
   c. psychologists.
   d. teachers.

   _____

   _____

2. Two statements that appeal to emotion are that
   a. the program would put your study habits to good use.
   b. it would be fun to experience college life first hand.
   c. you could learn advanced math.
   d. you could improve your science abilities.

   _____

   _____

3. Two statements that appeal to reason are that
   a. Jim Beiswenger seems like a nice person.
   b. the program helps students develop skills needed in college.
   c. it would be fun to visit Grand Falls.
   d. it has already helped over 100 health professionals in their education.

   _____

   _____

B. Write a persuasive letter that encourages the reader to support a needy cause or charity. Use details that appeal both to emotions and to reason. Begin your letter here.

   _____

   _____

   _____

   _____

   _____

Practicing Word Origins

A. Put an X next to the word or phrase that best completes each statement. Explain your answers on the lines provided.

1. The word *psychologist* comes from the Greek word *psyche,* meaning mind. Therefore, a *psychologist* is

   ____ a person who studies music.

   ____ someone who is learning about physics.

   ____ a person who studies how the mind works.

   ____ a student of philosophy.

   _____

2. The word *academic* comes from the word *akademia,* the name of the place where the Greek philosopher Plato taught. *Academic* probably means

   ____ having to do with schools or education.

   ____ philosophical.

   ____ platonic.

   ____ capable.

   _____

3. Another word that comes from *akademia* is

   ____ altruism.

   ____ acknowledgment.

   ____ alchemy.

   ____ academy.

   _____

B. Think of a word you have learned recently. Look it up in a dictionary. Tell the meaning of its root and from which language it came.

_____

_____

_____

_____

_____

_____

Applying *Word Origins*

Read the passage below. Then complete the items that follow.

> *Dear Fitness Enthusiast,*
>
> *It's the hottest trend in aerobics! It will build endurance, help you lose weight, and improve cardiovascular performance.*
>
> *What is it? It's "Boxing Fitness." It's for men. It's for women. It's for you!*
>
> *Aerobic boxing has additional benefits. It can relieve stress, improve eye-hand coordination, and strengthen upper body endurance.*
>
> *Call our facility today and make an appointment for a free lesson. We know you'll be so pleased with the results that you'll come back again and again.*
>
> *See you at the gymnasium!*

1. The word *cardiovascular* comes from the words *kardia*, meaning heart, and *vas*, meaning blood vessel. Based on this information, explain what *cardiovascular* performance probably means.

_____

_____

_____

_____

2. Use a dictionary to find the origin of the word *gymnasium*. From which languages does this word come?

_____

_____

_____

_____

3. List one other word that has the same root as *gymnasium*.

_____

_____

_____

_____

To review

↓

page
50

Indians into Medicine (INMED) is a health careers program serving Native American students from the seventh-grade level through professional school. Any Native American student with an interest in the health field is invited to contact INMED. As this letter indicates, attending the Summer Institute is one way to start taking advantage of INMED's many programs.

The notes in the margins show how one reader analyzed details that appeal to reason and emotion in the letter.

INDIANS INTO MEDICINE
"Center of Excellence"

INMED PROGRAM
UND SCHOOL OF MEDICINE
501 N. COLUMBIA ROAD
GRAND FORKS, ND 58203

Dear Student:

This paragraph tells who this letter is meant for—Indian students. I think the words *productive futures* make a strong appeal to reason.

The Indians into Medicine program offers health career opportunities to Indian students. Our program is very important, because many capable young Indians who could build productive futures for themselves in the health field do not even consider such careers. These same students are probably well aware of the need for more health professionals at many Indian reservations.

The first sentence in this paragraph appeals to Indian students' sense of pride. This is an emotional appeal.

We consider the Indian youth of today to be a pool of potential health professionals who deserve the opportunity to achieve the fulfilling careers they are capable of achieving. INMED has assisted over 100 medical doctors, nurses, psychologists and related health professionals during their educations, and we start working with students as young as seventh graders.

UND is an equal opportunity/affirmative action institution

INMED holds summer enrichment sessions each year for students in grades seven through 12 at which students can learn more about health careers, improve their math and science abilities, and develop the solid academic backgrounds to achieve in college courses.

The Summer Institute is a six-week program at the University of North Dakota campus in Grand Forks. Participants come from all over the country to experience college life first-hand at UND. We try to offer enriching and fun experiences for our participants, and many apply to return summer after summer.

Please consider putting your talents to an effective use by providing health care for Indian people. The INMED Summer Institute can help you learn more about the activities of a variety of health professionals. The Institute can also help you learn more about yourself.

Call an INMED counselor to find out more about our Summer Institute.

Sincerely,

Jim Beiswenger
Program Specialist

◀ Here are some more good reasons to consider the program. So far, I'd say this letter is balanced between appealing to reason and emotion.

Now write your own sidenotes. Look for details that appeal to reason and details that appeal to emotion.

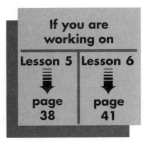

If you are working on

Lesson 5	Lesson 6
⬇	⬇
page 38	page 41

Quercus State College (QSC) is a small New Jersey college that attracts students from the surrounding states. With approximately 5,000 students, QSC specializes in education, nursing, and environmental studies. The letter below invites high school seniors to visit the college.

As you read, make notes in the margin that reflect your analysis of the persuasive techniques in the letter. Does the writer appeal to reason or to emotions?

QUERCUS STATE COLLEGE
SINCE 1910

"My visit to Quercus State College was like a dream come true. As I walked among the ivy-colored buildings, the giant oaks, and the friendly students... I knew that I had found another home!"

Students who visit Quercus State send back rave reviews with their applications. We are confident you will feel the same excitement as our many other visitors have felt. Because we care about you and your future, and because we are certain you will love our college, we are sending you a personal invitation to visit us this spring or summer.

Since you are faced with such an important decision, we know you want to ask questions regarding life on campus, degree programs, student activities, and more. We encourage you to speak openly with our Director of Admissions. She will greet you and your family as you arrive and will introduce you to a student ambassador who will show you the campus, discuss life at QSC, and answer any questions you have.

One of your main concerns, of course, is our academic program, so, if you wish, we will arrange for you to sit in on a class. This will give you a feeling for the atmosphere in our classes. Because we stress faculty-student interaction, we will arrange for you to meet with a faculty member. When you arrive on campus as a first-year student, you will participate in a Fall Orientation program directed by your faculty advisor. This program will give you a solid sense of confidence and of belonging. Your faculty advisor will work with you in planning your classes throughout your college years.

We know that daily life is another of your important concerns. We encourage you to visit the Student Center. Please stroll through our well-stocked bookstore, campus post office, and student lounges. For lunch you can enjoy a meal from the cafeteria or a snack from the deli. Your student ambassador will take you to visit a few dorm rooms, so that you will see the comfort and variety available. We are enclosing a brochure to help you plan your campus visit. We look forward to seeing you and your family.

Our most important role is to help you discover the warmth of our campus community. We realize QSC may be one of several candidates you are considering and we welcome the chance to show you our outstanding way of life and of learning. Inside the brochure you will find a reservation card. Please fill it out to arrange a visit you our campus. Give us a chance to share our warmth with you.

Best wishes to you in your senior year!

Sincerely,

Sandra DeJesús

Sandra DeJesús
Director of Admissions

QUERCUS STATE COLLEGE

RIVERDELL, NEW JERSEY

Reviewing Reading Persuasive Letters

A. Read the letter from Quercus State College on pages 46-47. As you read, circle details that appeal to the reader's emotions and underline details that appeal to reason. Select some of the most important details that you circled. Use them to complete the chart below.

Details that Appeal to Reason

+

Details that Appeal to Emotions

Reader's Response
Were persuasive techniques effective?

B. Imagine that you have chosen a school or program in which to continue your education. Write a letter to the Admissions Officer persuading him or her to accept you as a student.

Testing *Reading Persuasive Letters*

A. The statements below are based on the letter from Quercus State College on pages 46-47. Write the letter E before statements that appeal mainly to the emotions and the letter R before statements that appeal mainly to reason. Then explain your answer on the lines provided.

1. ___ "As I walked among the ivy-covered buildings, the giant oaks, and the friendly students. . . I knew that I had found my college home!"

_____

_____

2. ___ "You are faced with an important decision. We know you want to ask questions regarding life on campus, degree programs, students activities, and more."

_____

_____

3. ___ "When you arrive on campus as a Freshman, you will participate in a Fall Orientation program directed by your personal faculty advisor."

_____

_____

4. ___ "Our most important role is to help you discover the warmth of our campus community."

_____

_____

B. Does the QSC letter appeal mainly to reason or to emotion? Do you think it is effective as a persuasive letter? Why or why not?

_____

_____

_____

_____

_____

_____

To begin Lesson 6 ⇊ **page 41**

Reviewing *Word Origins*

A. Reread the letter from Quercus State College on pages 46-47. Choose one of the words you circled and look up its origin in the dictionary.

Word:
_____

Definition:
_____

Root:
_____

Meaning of the Root Word:
_____

Other Words That Come from the Root Word:
_____

B. Write a paragraph using the words you added to the bottom box of the chart.

_____

_____

_____

_____

_____

_____

_____

_____

_____

_____

_____

_____

Testing Word Origins

A. The incomplete statements below are based on the letter on pages 46-47. Fill in the oval next to the words or phrases that best complete each statement. Then on the lines provided, explain why you chose your answer.

1. The word *snack* comes from the older English word *snaken. Snaken* most likely means
   ○ to be shaped like a snake.
   ○ to shrink.
   ○ to bite.
   ○ to go without food.

   _____

   _____

2. The word *campus* comes directly from the Latin word *campus,* which means field or plain. Another English word that has the same origin is
   ○ campaign.
   ○ campsite.
   ○ camshaft.
   ○ camouflage.

   _____

   _____

3. The origin of the word *candidate* is the Latin word *candidatus,* which means clothed in white. Romans running for office wore white to show they were honest and pure. Another word with the same origin is
   ○ candle.
   ○ candor.
   ○ honesty.
   ○ candy.

   _____

   _____

B. In a sentence, tell what courses a person would need in order to become an engineer. Then choose a word from the sentence and use a dictionary to discover its origin. Explain the word's origin in a second sentence.

   _____

   _____

Unit FOUR

BECOMING AN ACTIVE READER

Good readers are active readers. When they read **advertorials** they look forward to learning new ideas and to being entertained. Good readers also like to tell friends and family members about what they have read and why they did or did not enjoy reading it.

Using Skills and Strategies

Asking questions can help you identify the **author's purpose** for writing an advertorial. You might ask: Is the writer trying to amuse or entertain me? Is he or she trying to convince me to act or behave in a certain way? Is the writer providing me with new information on a topic?

Identifying **main ideas** in an advertorial is another strategy readers can use to read actively. As you read, ask: What major ideas are presented? What **details** does the author use to support the main idea?

In this unit, the skills of identifying the **author's purpose** and determining **main ideas and details** will help you become an active reader.

Reading the Advertorial

An advertorial is similar to an advertisement in that it promotes a product, service, or consumer opportunity. Like advertisements, advertorials are paid for by their sponsors. But advertorials are also like editorials in that they use facts and opinions to convince readers to buy the services or products they discuss. Advertorials appear in magazines and newspapers and are usually designed to attract a reader's attention.

Responding to Advertorials

Good readers respond to advertorials by analyzing the main points being made. Jot down your reactions in the side margins as you read the advertorials "New York City Off the Beaten Path" and "Come Celebrate the Harvest Moon Festival." Use your notes when you discuss the selections with your classmates.

Author's Purpose

Introducing Strategies

An advertorial is a type of advertisement consisting mostly of words. In an advertorial, the **author's purpose** is to sell a product, service, or location. To do this, the writer persuades, entertains, informs, or shares an experience with the reader. Good readers ask themselves, "Does this information persuade me to buy the product or service? Am I influenced by the writer's enthusiasm? Is the information unique?" Knowing the author's purpose helps readers make judgments about the writer's ideas.

Remembering the steps in the chart below can help you read advertorials carefully and analyze the author's purpose for writing.

Reading Advertorials

Read "NEW YORK CITY Off the Beaten Path" on pages 59-63 and the sidenotes on pages 59-61. The sidenotes show how one good reader identified the author's purpose and analyzed his persuasive techniques. After you finish reading, complete the items below.

1. What are some of the informational and persuasive details that helped the reader identify the author's purpose?

_____

_____

2. Give an example of how the reader responded to an informational or persuasive statement.

_____

Practicing Author's Purpose

A. Each incomplete statement below is based on "NEW YORK CITY Off the Beaten Path" on pages 59-63. Place an X next to the words that best complete each statement. Then on the lines provided, explain your choice.

1. The author's main purpose is to

_____ tell stories about fictional New Yorkers.

_____ interest people in visiting New York City.

_____

_____

2. Because the author wants to publicize New York City's attractions, he does not

_____ describe interesting off-beat things to do.

_____ write about crime in the city.

_____

_____

3. When the author writes, "Just being in Manhattan makes you feel ready to take on the world," he is

_____ appealing to the reader's sense of adventure.

_____ stating an important fact about the city.

_____

_____

4. One detail that gives information about the city's cultural attractions is that

_____ the National Museum of the American Indian houses the world's largest collection of Indian art.

_____ people shouldn't be shy about haggling in the clothing shops on Canal Street.

_____

_____

B. Do you think the advertorial achieved the author's purpose? Why or why not? Write your personal response to the advertorial in the space below.

_____

_____

Applying *Author's Purpose*

Read the excerpt below from an advertising supplement to the October 10, 1993 *New York Times Magazine*. After you read the advertorial, answer the questions that follow.

A TASTE OF ITALY

Italian food, Italian style, the charisma of Italy have enraptured America. The proliferation of Italian restaurants and casual eateries, the plethora of imported Italian-made products on the shelves of supermarkets and gourmet shops is vivid proof of this love affair with all that is Italian.

Unfortunately, American consumers who rummage through gastronomic selections. . . which bear Italian-sounding names [can be misled]. . . . Our recommendation: be a judicious buyer. When confronted with a myriad of Italian-sounding names. . . look for. . . the words "Made in Italy" "Product of Italy". . . on the label. . . . Demand the very best. . . . Buon Appetito!

1. What does the writer hope the reader will do after reading this selection?

_____

_____

2. How does the writer try to achieve this purpose? Include details from the text to explain your answer.

_____

_____

B. Write a brief advertorial for a product or service directed toward a specific audience. To persuade your readers, use details that entertain as well as inform.

_____

_____

_____

_____

_____

_____

_____

To review

↓

page
70

Main Idea and Details

| *Lesson 8* | Introducing page 56 | Practicing page 57 | Applying page 58 | Reviewing page 72 | Testing page 73 |

Introducing Strategies

Good readers look for main ideas as they read. They note the **main idea** for each paragraph or section of an article. Then they review these main ideas to determine the central idea or thread that runs through the whole article. The main idea of one section, for example, may turn out to be an important detail that tells about the central idea of the entire article.

The chart below shows how readers can keep track of the main ideas in an article to determine the author's central idea.

| CENTRAL IDEA |

| Main Detail |

Detail 1
Detail 2

| Main Detail |

Detail 1
Detail 2

Reading the Advertorial

Reread "NEW YORK CITY Off the Beaten Path" on pages 59-64. As you read, underline some of the main ideas the writer is making. Think about how they support the writer's central idea.

1. List one or two of the main ideas you identified in each section of the advertorial.

_____

_____

2. Write a central idea statement for the whole advertorial based on the points you listed above.

_____

_____

Practicing *Main Idea and Details*

A. Read each statement below about "NEW YORK CITY Off the Beaten Path." If the statement tells about a main idea from the advertorial, write a sentence underneath that provides a supporting detail. If the statement contains a supporting detail, write a sentence that states its main idea.

1. Chinatown has plenty of *dim sum* restaurants.

_____

_____

2. New York City has plays, concerts, food, shopping, and museums to suit everyone's tastes.

_____

_____

3. It's the off-beat side of New York that is the best part of the city to visit.

_____

_____

4. You can walk along St. Mark's Place and find out what's the fashionable color to dye your hair these days.

_____

_____

B. Write an outline for an advertorial about the place where you live or would like to live. Include main idea statements that would support your central idea. Add some details that support the main ideas.

_____

_____

_____

_____

_____

_____

_____

Applying *Main Idea and Details*

Read the excerpt below from *Adventures in Travel*, a supplement to the October 24th, 1993, *New York Times*, by Alison Arnett. After you read it, answer the questions that follow.

VITAL SIGNS

In the jumble of the Santo Domingo streets, the man's concentration was striking. He lay on a make-shift platform carefully painting dresses and shoes onto the plaster wall . . . .

Such practical art appears all over the Dominican Republic . . . . A big camera for a camera shop . . . washing machines for an appliance store . . . colored fish for a pet shop.

Argelia Tejada, a Dominican sociologist, explains it as a way for small businesses to advertise music and all the arts are vital to the Latin cultures, she says, and the wall-painted signs are just another way to incorporate art into daily life.

1. Write a statement that explains the purpose of wall art on the streets of the Dominican Republic.

_____

_____

2. In the first paragraph of the selection, how does the description of the artist's work contribute to the main idea?

_____

_____

3. What examples of "practical art" are mentioned?

_____

_____

B. Write a paragraph describing an attraction in your community or in a city or town you have visited. State your feeling about the subject as the central idea. Give some details that support your central idea.

To review
↓
page
72

_____

_____

_____

_____

The notes in the margins on pages 59-61 show how one reader thought about the author's purpose and persuasive techniques while reading the advertorial about New York City.

SPECIAL ADVERTISING SECTION

NEW YORK CITY
Off the Beaten Path

◄ The title and the words *Special Advertising Section* at the top tell me this article is an advertorial about New York City.

by Joseph D'O'Brian

The best thing about New York is that thrill it gives you. Just being in Manhattan makes you feel ready to take on the world. And as often as not, you'll find it's the off-beat side of the city that gives you that thrill.

◄ The writer tells the reader about the "thrill" that being in New York City gives you. I'll try not to let the writer's enthusiasm influence me, but it seems like a fun article.

Most people come here with a standard list of things to see and do. And, granted, most of what the natives refer to as "the touristy stuff" is worth seeing and doing. But once you've been to Yankee Stadium, the Statue of Liberty, and the Empire State Building, you can start in on the best part of your visit to New York City: the things you don't know about until you've been here awhile.

Just being in Manhattan makes you feel ready to take on the world.

It'll take a little digging to discover some of our best-loved secrets. But here are a few suggestions to help you on your journey.

◄ I think the purpose of this ad is to tell tourists about New York's "best-loved secrets."

Theatre—More Than Broadway

It's fun to take in a Broadway show. There's something very "native" about hanging around the half-price ticket booth on Times Square and seeing what's available. But Broadway is just a small part of the picture. If you want to see real New York theatre—that is, the kind of theatre that's part of our everyday life here—head for "Off-Off-Broadway."

The backbone of the New York theatre scene is the network of tiny "black box" theatres scattered around

◄ I can see by the headings *Theatre, Dining, Shopping, Museums,* and *Things,* he's talking about attractions in any city. But what makes this advertorial different are words like "If you want to see real New York theatre"—I'm being made to feel like an insider.

▶ Chelsea, Greenwich Village, SoHo, and TriBeCa, plus the stretch of Forty-second Street between Ninth and Tenth Avenues known as "Theatre Row." On any given night, you can choose from a classical production of Shakespeare or Sophocles, a modern treatment of a three-hundred-year-old Restoration comedy, an experimental drama by a promising young author, a musical that might or might not make it to Broadway, or a one-man show by someone who wrote, directed, acted, and produced the whole thing.

The backbone of the New York theatre scene is the network of tiny "black box" theatres scattered around Chelsea, Greenwich Village, SoHo, and TriBeCa.

To find out what's available around town, check any of the weekly papers or magazines that cover the local entertainment scene: The "Off-Off-Broadway" listings will give you a choice of as many as fifty shows.

If you're a fan of modern dance, it's the same story: A dance recital at Lincoln Center is sure to be a great experience, but you might also wander downtown for an experimental performance at one-tenth the cost.

Those same newspaper

▶ and magazine listings will usually include sections headed "Performance Art" and "Spoken Word." The former could be anything: a multi-media show, dance, mime, improvisation, guerrilla theatre, or a little of each. As for the latter, who says nobody reads poetry any more? Various small clubs and restaurants throughout the city, mainly in the East Village, are

Fans of rock, jazz, and experimental music will think they've gone to heaven when they're in New York.

proving grounds for today's up-and-coming poets; you'll also hear recitals of classic poetry.

Fans of rock, jazz, and experimental music will think they've gone to heaven when they're in New York. The area bounded by Fourth and Houston Streets, between Sixth Avenue and The Bowery, is the neighborhood for anything from straight-ahead jazz to rockabilly to heavy metal. A night of club-crawling here is a must.

Dining—Savory Surprises

If you were to ask your average New Yorker what's the best thing about living here, the answer's most likely to be "Food." It's inescapable. Practically anywhere you walk, the dominant scent will be of something cooking. If it's eaten anywhere in the world, you can get it in New York.

Different neighborhoods in the city have different specialties. Choose one and wander until you find the restaurant that looks, smells, and feels right. It won't take long.

Little India, on East Sixth Street between First and Second Avenues, is a popular spot for the adventurous. The block is lined with Indian and Pakistani restaurants, all good, all . . . cheap, serving up hot lamb curry, tandoori chicken, vegetarian casseroles, delicious native breads, creamy rich desserts, and refreshing Indian beer.

For heartier, less spicy dishes, Little Ukrainia is just two minutes away. This is a short stretch of Second Avenue, centered around East Ninth Street. If your roots are in Eastern Europe, you'll feel right at home here.

Most visitors know about Chinatown, but few know about dim sum. This is the traditional

> Indian and Pakistani restaurants serve up hot lamb curry, vegetarian casseroles, and delicious native breads.

I think if I were planning a trip to New York I'd find this article very helpful—and convincing. It's usually the off-beat, out-of-the-way attractions that are the most fun.

I hope the author is going to give details about sports in New York, because that's one thing that would really make me want to visit the city.

All this talk of food is making my mouth water; but the author is also giving a lot of information about the kinds of food available in different neighborhoods.

Write your own sidenotes as you read the rest of the article. Note details that helped you determine the author's purpose.

Chinese lunch, at which carts loaded with various exotic small dishes (usually dumplings) are wheeled past your table. You take whatever looks good; when you're done, the waiter counts up your empty plates and charges you accordingly. Chinatown has plenty of dim sum restaurants: You know you've found one if you see waiters pushing carts around the dining room. These restaurants are usually crowded, so arrive early, be prepared to wait, and expect to share your table.

> **Second Avenue in the Eighties is Manhattan's Hungarian enclave.**

Second Avenue in the Eighties is Manhattan's Hungarian enclave, with not only some terrific restaurants, but also a couple of gourmet shops that specialize in Central European delicacies.

If you happen to be in the neighborhood of Rockefeller Center around lunchtime, take a walk over to Sixth Avenue at West Fiftieth Street. Thousands of New Yorkers have their lunch outside here when the weather's nice, and no wonder. We love "street food," and on this corner you can take your pick of Chinese, Japanese, Israeli, Thai, Afghan, Italian, and Greek cuisine, and a few others besides—all sold from pushcarts.

Shopping—Do It by Neighborhood

Shopping is a close second to eating on most New Yorkers' list of pastimes. Everyone knows about Fifth Avenue and the major department stores. But to find the real bargains, and the real out-of-the-way merchandise, try some of these neighborhoods:

> **Most shops [on Bleeker Street are] . . . treasure troves of folk art, lighting, clothing, jewelry, toys, vintage paintings, and sculptures.**

ANTIQUES: From the corner of Seventh Avenue, wander west on Bleecker Street. Browsing along this quarter-mile stretch, you'll probably want to redecorate your home several times over. Some of the antique shops here are pretty pricey (but worth it); others offer "fixer-upper" furniture at bargain prices. Most shops have their specialties: besides furniture, they're treasure troves of folk art, lighting, clothing, jewelry, toys, vintage paintings and sculptures, and objects such as walking sticks, pens, and cigarette cases.

It's not all antiques: This neighborhood is also one of the best in the city for artistic ceramics and glassware, high-fashion clothing, the latest in men's and women's hairstyling, and off-beat art galleries.

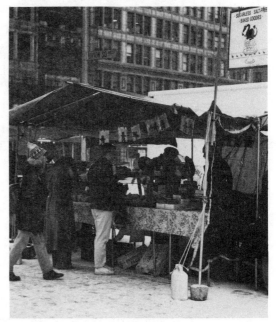

OUTDOOR MARKETS: After having lunch in Chinatown, wander along Canal Street from the Bowery to West Broadway. Most of the stores here are open-fronted; even the enclosed ones have a flea-market feel to them. The merchandise changes as you walk along the north side of Canal Street: Near the Bowery, you'll find almost nothing but jewelry stores; further west, the stores specialize in fake name-brand watches and pens, costume jewelry, and souvenirs; as you approach West Broadway you'll see numerous electronics and hardware stores. On the south side of Canal, it's mainly clothing and luggage. Don't be shy about haggling: A smart negotiator will walk away happy.

> **The city has several permanent flea markets, mainly in SoHo and Greenwich Village; the best-known is held on weekends on Broadway between Fourth and Great Jones Streets.**

The city has several permanent flea markets, mainly in SoHo and Greenwich Village; the best-known is held on weekends on Broadway between Fourth and Great Jones Streets.

Museums—Well Kept Secrets

It's impossible to get an accurate count of museums in New York City, because new ones open up all the time. Once you've hit the "must-sees" (the Met, MoMA, the

Guggenheim, the Museum of Natural History), try some of the lesser-known ones.

The Children's Museum of Manhattan, on Eighty-third Street between Broadway and Amsterdam Avenue, is ideal for children under ten. Most of its exhibits are more than just things to look at: They require participation and involve all the senses. The museum's attractions on weekends also include puppet shows, storytelling, theatre, and music.

Located at Twenty-five West Fifty-second Street, The Museum of Television and Radio covers the eighty-year history of radio and TV.

Located at Twenty-five West Fifty-second Street, The Museum of Television and Radio covers the eighty-year history of radio and TV. You can hear and see tapes of more than 40,000 radio and TV programs in private screening booths, or see public screenings.

The National Museum of the American Indian, on Broadway and One-hundred-and-fifty-fifth Street, houses the world's largest collection of Indian art and artifacts.

Things We Don't Notice

New York's also full of little pleasures that the locals take for granted and that visitors don't know about. Like standing at the front window of the first car of a subway train, getting a motorman's eye-view of the route; hanging out in Washington Square Park on a Saturday afternoon and checking out the jugglers, singers, and stand-up comics, doing their bits for whatever change they can get; walking along St. Mark's Place in the East Village to find out what's the fashionable color to dye your hair these days; or sitting at a sidewalk cafe on Columbus Avenue, any evening, just watching the natives go by. It's these little things that make you pinch yourself and say, "Hey! You're in New York!" *Advertisement*

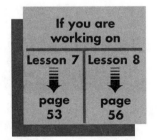

If you are working on

Lesson 7	Lesson 8
⬇	⬇
page 53	page 56

ADVERTISEMENT

Come Celebrate the Harvest Moon Festival

by Angela Chen

You probably thought the smiling moon face in Chinese folklore is a man in the moon, but take a closer peek. The face is really a woman with two friends: a rabbit and a toad.

Once a year, Chinese people all over the world celebrate the Asian myth of this woman in the moon. The observance is a ritual carried forward through thousands of years of Chinese tradition. This year, you're invited to join the fun as Chinatown gears up to enjoy the Harvest Moon Festival. If any visitors leave without experiencing Chinatown or the Harvest Moon Festival, they have not really experienced San Francisco.

> **If any visitors leave without experiencing Chinatown or the Harvest Moon Festival, they have not really experienced San Francisco.**

Harvest Moon occurs the 15th day of the eighth month of the Chinese lunar calendar (in September or October by the Western calendar). It is sometimes described as Thanksgiving Day for people of Chinese descent. It is a holiday during which families come together, farmers celebrate a successful harvest, and people count their blessings and honor the dead.

According to Chinese beliefs, the moon influences crops. At harvest time, when the moon is full, the moon is especially revered. It is at this time, when the moon is brightest, that the Harvest Moon festival occurs. The positioning of the moon is a key to the holiday. The moon must be at its farthest point from the Earth. When that happens, the Chinese then say, "she is perfectly round." This is the Day of the Moon.

Bustle Over the Moon in Chinatown

Even on regular days, San Francisco's Chinatown is a busy place. Its lively atmosphere—crowded streets, colorful shops, authentic restaurants—allows the visitor to gain a real "feel" for the culture.

On the Day of the Moon, the busy streets and alleys of Chinatown become even more crowded. During this time of the year, you can experience some special traditions. For example, toy shops sell the figure of a solemn-looking Chinese official seated on a chair and clothed in a red and green garment. Yet, there's something different about this figure. It has a pair of long, thin white ears! He is the "Moon Hare," an inhabitant of the moon.

As part of the festivities, schools, businesses, and associations march the streets of Chinatown in a long procession. The Lion Dance, performed by many different troupes known as Lion Dancers, opens the celebration. Each troupe consists of several members who hold the brightly colored cloth lion over their heads. One person holds the cardboard head while another holds the tail. The Lion Dancers display remarkable skill and agility, showing that they are among the greatest dancers in the world. The lion's eyeballs, tongue, jaw, ears, and tail move rapidly, while the bells of the neck collars tinkle along with the beat of gongs.

> **" The Lion Dance, performed by many different troupes known as Lion Dancers, opens the celebration. "**

During the march, the year's beauty queen, or Miss Chinatown, also appears. Sometimes she and other women perform special moon-watching ceremonies based on ancient rituals.

Get Your Sweet Tooth Ready!

One of the characteristics that sets this holiday apart from others is the food associated with it. Most important is the "moon cake," the chief symbol of this special occasion.

The moon cake is a small cake made in the shape of the moon and baked to a golden brown. It is about one inch thick and is stuffed with a mixture of sweetened soya beans, lotus seeds, and whole egg yolks. It is the tastiest treat you could ever give yourself. Although moon cakes are available throughout the year in Chinatown bakeries, it is on the Day of the Moon that they become special as well as symbolic. Preserved duck egg yolks, representing the full moon, are often placed in the center of the fillings. The cakes are marked with one, two, three, or four red dots to indicate the number of duck eggs inside. They also are often decorated with pictures of the Moon Hare or the Moon Toad.

Moon cakes have a special place in Chinese history. In the 14th century, moon cakes were the means of getting secret instructions to Chinese patriots who were under the control of the Mongol dynasty. The Mongolians placed a man in every Chinese household. This man closely watched all family members and expected them to bow to his will. Communication was not allowed between patriots. Then an unknown Chinese person hit upon the idea of writing secret messages on little paper squares that could be tucked inside moon cakes. When the cakes were sent, as they still are, from neighbor to neighbor and friend to friend, the pastries carried secret messages. An attack on the Mongolians was planned in this way. The surprise attack succeeded, and the revolt led to the overthrow of the tyrants.

" Moon cakes were the means of getting secret instructions to Chinese patriots "

Accompanying the moon cakes at traditional Harvest Moon celebrations is the pomelo. This is a fruit similar to the grapefruit, except that a pomelo is twice as large and very sweet. Unfortunately, pomelos grown in California are fairly sour. Therefore, substitutes such as apples and oranges are used in this country.

But these are not all of the sweet treats you can find during the Harvest Moon Festival. Look for little figures of rabbits and other animals that are made from candied sugar. You can also find animal-shaped cookies. To help you digest all of these delicacies, drink lots of hot tea. But make sure it's Chinese tea—the best in the world.

History of the Celebration: A Festival for Ladies

Myths and stories about the Harvest Moon Festival vary from country to country, but the most popular legend goes something like this:

The Goddess Ch'ang O is the moon's most highly regarded inhabitant. She fled to the moon after eating the herb of immortality. Her husband, an archer named Hou-I, gave the herb to her after he saved the Earth by shooting down nine of ten suns. . . .

After this point, the myth has many versions. However, the ending remains the same among storytellers: The Goddess becomes the master of the moon and her husband becomes the master of the sun.

This is why the Chinese Harvest Moon Festival is a ladies' tradition. In Chinese mythology, the moon is a feminine symbol with the qualities of gentleness, quietness, and darkness, among others. Not surprisingly, the moon is the protector of women. As the tradition goes, in every family it is the duty of the women to worship the moon. A Chinese proverb says: "Men must not worship the Moon."

In describing the hour when the moon is clear, Chinese myth states, "Poor homes are changed into places of enchantment because Ch'ang O touches them with her silver fingers. She hides

❝ Myths and stories about the Harvest Moon Festival vary from country to country ❞

❝The Harvest Moon Festival still attracts people from all walks of life. What keeps them coming back yearly is the sweet aroma of the moon cakes.❞

the poverty and wipes the wrinkles from tired faces."

In old China, women regularly worshipped the Goddess of the Moon. Two candles were lit and bundles of incense sticks were placed in the family urn. The ceremony lasted a few minutes, concluding with the posting of a picture of the Moon Rabbit. After bowing to the picture, the women took it down and burned it.

In former days in the United States, some Chinese American families performed the ceremony of honoring the moon in a different way. They placed moon cakes, fruits, and lighted incense sticks outside on a table. Then, at the stroke of midnight, when the moon became full, the family "captured" the moon by catching its reflection in a basin of water. This ceremony is mostly forgotten today, however.

Contemporary Ceremony: Simplified, Yet Fun

Today, Chinese American men and women celebrate the Harvest Moon by taking the day off and gathering family members for a good dinner. The meal ends, of course, with the enjoyment of luscious moon cakes. The social activities are decided among family members, but often the evening is devoted to moon-viewing parties.

Many centuries since it began, the Harvest Moon Festival still attracts people from all walks of life. Most people, including the Chinese Americans of recent generations, are uncertain about the festival's origins, but what keeps them coming back yearly is the sweet aroma of the moon cakes.

This year, visit Chinatown during the Harvest Moon Festival. Take a friend with you—it's the best day he or she could ever spend. Go and enjoy this mysterious Chinese folk tradition!

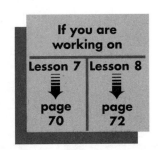

If you are working on

Lesson 7	Lesson 8
⬇	⬇
page 70	page 72

Reviewing *Author's Purpose*

A. Read the selection "Come Celebrate the Harvest Moon Festival" on pages 64-69. As you read, circle words that give clues about the author's purpose. Underline informative and persuasive details that you responded to as you read. Use the information to complete the chart below.

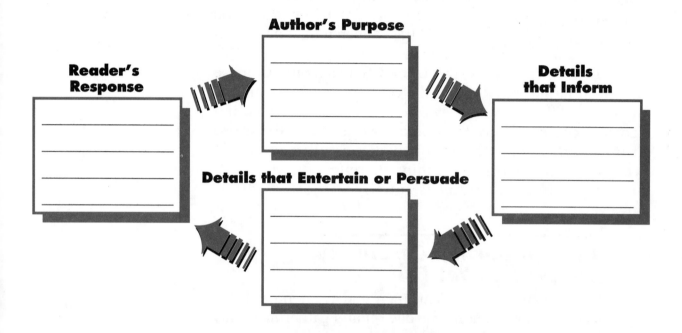

Author's Purpose

Reader's Response

Details that Inform

Details that Entertain or Persuade

B. What parts of the Harvest Moon Festival most appeal to you? Write a paragraph telling what you would most want to see and do on that day. Use details from the advertorial in your paragraph.

Testing *Author's Purpose*

A. The statements below are based on "Come Celebrate the Harvest Moon Festival" on pages 64-69. Fill in the oval next to each statement that you think identifies a purpose for writing the advertorial. Then on the lines provided, explain your answers.

○ The author wants people to visit San Francisco's Chinatown during the Harvest Moon celebration.

_____

_____

○ The author is trying to teach people about the history of San Francisco.

_____

_____

○ The author provides background information about the origins of the Harvest Moon Festival to interest people in attending.

_____

_____

○ The author talks about moon cakes because they play an important part in the festival and because most people are interested in foods connected to holidays.

_____

_____

B. Write an advertorial about a celebration. Your purpose in writing is to persuade people to attend the celebration.

_____

_____

_____

_____

_____

_____

To begin
Lesson 8

page
56

Unit FIVE

BECOMING AN ACTIVE READER

Good readers read actively. When they read **poems** and listen to **songs**, they want to be entertained and inspired. Good readers discover their own thoughts and feelings through poetry and songs.

Using Skills and Strategies

Comparing and **contrasting** the form and content of poems and songs will help you read for enjoyment. You might ask: Are the forms of the poems different? Are the poems similar in content? Do different images come to mind as I read or listen to the song?

Looking for relationships among words is another way to read poems and songs actively. Poets often use related words that can be made into **analogies**. In an analogy, poets compare ideas by showing the relationships between words.

In this unit, **comparing and contrasting** and constructing **analogies** will help you become an active reader.

Poetry: The Poet's Voice

Poems often express the poet's deepest feelings and emotions. Songs are similar to poems in that many are poetry set to music. People of all cultures write and enjoy poetry and songs. By reading these two very personal forms of literature, readers can experience the similarities in the feelings and emotions among people of all cultures.

Responding to Poetry and Songs

Good readers experience the emotions of poets by putting themselves "inside" the poem or the song. It is important to jot down your responses in the side margins as you read the poems and the songs in this unit. Writing sidenotes will help you become involved in what you read. Use your notes to discuss the poems with your classmates.

Compare and Contrast

Introducing Strategies

Good readers become involved as they read by making connections among ideas, thoughts, and feelings. They **compare and contrast** the author's or poet's style, point of view, or mood with something they have already read. The next time you read a poem, for example, ask yourself: What does this poem remind me of? Is the point of view the same as something else I have read? How is it different? Are both poems written in rhyme or in free verse?

The diagram below shows one way you can compare and contrast poems as you read.

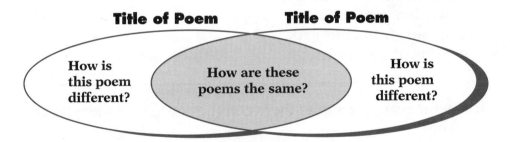

Title of Poem   **Title of Poem**

How is this poem different?   How are these poems the same?   How is this poem different?

Reading the Poems

Read the poems "On the Spirit of Mildred Jordan" and "The Lost Daughter" on pages 81-83. Use the poems and the sidenotes to complete the items below. The sidenotes show how one good reader compared and contrasted form, content, point of view, and mood in the two poems.

1. List two comparisons that the reader made about the poems.

_____

_____

2. List two contrasts that the reader found in the poems.

_____

_____

Practicing Compare and Contrast

A. The following statements are about similarities and differences in the poems "On the Spirit of Mildred Jordan" and "The Lost Daughter." Circle the letter next to the words that best complete each statement. Then, on the line provided, tell why you made that choice.

1. The poems can be compared in form because they both
   a. use free verse.
   b. have five stanzas.
   c. are told in the first person.
   d. all of the above

   _____

2. One important way in which the two poems compare in content is that they are both
   a. memories from early childhood.
   b. written by women.
   c. about strong mothers.
   d. none of the above

   _____

3. One important contrast between the content of the poems is that
   a. one poem directly states the fears and worries of the speaker, and the other does not.
   b. one poem is told by a daughter, and the other is not.
   c. one poem describes a mother's appearance, and the other does not.
   d. none of the above

   _____

B. On the lines below, list another way in which the content of both poems is alike and another way in which it is different.

   _____

   _____

   _____

   _____

   _____

Applying *Compare and Contrast*

A. Read the poem below. Then answer the questions that follow.

GRANDMOTHER

She walks with me along the street.
Frail legs unsure, stumbling feet.
Her back so bent. Was it always so?
The hesitation, movement slow.
Where is the girl that smiled at me
From pictures framed so lovingly?
The eyes that shined and laughed like mine.
Now dim with age and heartless time.

1. Compare and contrast the form of this poem to either "On the Spirit of Mildred Jordan" or "The Lost Daughter." Tell how the two poems are alike or different.

_____

_____

_____

_____

2. How are the two poems alike in content?

_____

_____

_____

_____

3. What contrasts do you find in the content of the two poems?

_____

_____

_____

_____

B. Write an additional two lines for the poem. Remember to be consistent in form and content.

_____

_____

_____

To review
page 87

Analogies

Introducing Strategies

Poets think carefully about their choice of words and the relationships among words. Good readers look for word relationships as they read. They know that noticing word relationships can help them read for a deeper appreciation of a poet's ideas. An **analogy** is one way of comparing ideas by showing relationships between words. The analogy below contains words from the poems "On the Spirit of Mildred Jordan" and "The Lost Daughter." The analogy is written first as a sentence, and then in a style you may have seen on tests.

oxfords **IS TO** shoes	**AS** a cloche **IS TO** a hat.
oxfords : shoes	:: cloche : hat

In an analogy, the first two words are related in the same way as the second two words: If oxfords are a type of shoes, then a cloche must be a type of hat. Other relationships that can be shown by analogies include:

- **part and whole** *(tree : forest :: mountain : range)*;
- **characteristics** *(swift : falcon :: agile : monkey)*;
- **opposites** *(knowledge : ignorance :: forgiveness : revenge)*;
- **similar meanings** *(poor : destitute :: wealthy : prosperous)*;
- **action to object** *(hoist : crane :: pry : crowbar)*; and
- **living thing and its place** *(eagle : aerie :: hare : burrow)*.

Reading the Poems

Reread the poems "On the Spirit of Mildred Jordan" and "The Lost Daughter." Circle and draw arrows between related words in each poem. Then complete the analogy below with a word from "On the Spirit of Mildred Jordan," and name the relationship.

1. sickness : healthiness :: feeble: _____

2. Relationship: _____

Practicing Analogies

A. Circle the letter next to the word that best completes each analogy. Then, on the line provided, write the relationship on which the analogy is based.

1. tacky : gum :: shiny : _____
   a. glow   b. brilliant
   c. rhinestone   d. powder
   Relationship: _____

2. foxy : _____ :: baggy : slack
   a. humorous   b. stingy
   c. lean   d. cunning
   Relationship: _____

3. taxi : vehicle :: muskrat : _____
   a. rodent   b. clothing
   c. alive   d. reptile
   Relationship: _____

4. _____ : ample :: thinned : thickened
   a. plenty   b. skimpy
   c. excess   d. massive
   Relationship: _____

5. float : parade :: _____ : store
   a. building   b. shopping
   c. merchandise   d. market
   Relationship: _____

B. You can better understand how analogies work if you write an analogy of your own. Select a word from one of the poems. Use the word to make up an analogy. Write the analogy in the diagram below:

_____ : _____ :: _____ : _____

Applying Analogies

A. Read the poem below by Emily Dickinson (1830-1886). Use one of the underlined words from the poem to complete each analogy that follows. Then list the relationship upon which the analogy is based.

> *This is my letter to the World*
> *That never wrote to Me—*
> *The simple News that Nature told—*
> *With tender Majesty*
>
> *Her Message is committed*
> *To Hands I cannot see—*
> *For love of Her—Sweet—countrymen—*
> *Judge tenderly—of Me*
>
> — Emily Dickinson

1. entrusted : _____ :: simple : uncomplicated

Relationship: _____

2. callously : harshly :: _____ : humanely

Relationship: _____

3. _____ : triviality :: love : animosity

Relationship: _____

4. professors : university :: _____ : nation

Relationship: _____

5. consume : food :: transmit : _____

Relationship: _____

6. _____ : mind :: write : hands

Relationship: _____

B. Choose another word from the poem. Use it in an analogy of your own.

_____ : _____ :: _____ : _____

To review

↓

page 89

June Jordan is a professor of African American studies and Women's Studies at the University of California in Berkeley. She has published more than a dozen books of poetry. The poem below, written about her mother, is from a 1977 collection of Jordan's poems titled *Things That I Do in the Dark.*

On the Spirit of Mildred Jordan

by June Jordan

After sickness and a begging
from her bed
my mother dressed herself
grey lace-up oxfords
stockings baggy on her shrunken legs
an orange topper
rhinestone buttons
and a powder blue straw
hat with plastic
flowers

Then
she took the street
in short steps toward the corner

chewing gum
no less

she let the family laugh
again

she wasn't foxy
she was strong

The notes in the margin show how one reader compared and contrasted the form of "On the Spirit of Mildred Jordan" to the form of "The Lost Daughter." Add to these notes as you read. Use the wide margin to write your own notes about how the poems are alike and different.

◄ "On the Spirit of Mildred Jordan" has five stanzas—one long one and four short ones. "The Lost Daughter" also has five stanzas, but each stanza has the same number of lines.

◄ Both poems are written in free verse—without a regular beat or rhyme. That's another way that the poems are alike.

◄ "On the Spirit of Mildred Jordan" doesn't use punctuation, but "The Lost Daughter" uses all the regular punctuation marks.

Marilyn Nelson Waniek is a professor of English at the University of Connecticut. She writes poetry for adults and children and has won many awards for her writing. The poem below, from her book titled *Mama's Promises*, also appears in *Double Stitch*, a 1991 collection of literature by African American women who have written about their mothers.

The Lost Daughter

by Marilyn Nelson Waniek

The notes in the margin show how one reader compared and contrasted the content of this poem to the poem "On the Spirit of Mildred Jordan." As you read, use the wide margins to make your own notes about how the content of the poems is alike and different.

Both these poems are about mothers. Both describe what the mothers are wearing, and the mothers in the poems seem very important to the narrators.

One morning just before Christmas
when I was four or five years old
I followed Mama's muskrat coat
and her burgundy cloche
from counter to counter in The May Co.
as she tested powders and colognes,
smoothed silk scarves and woolen vests,
and disappeared down the aisle
▶ into the life she lived before I was born.

The mirrors rendered nothing more
at my eye level than a small brown blur;
I understood why the salesclerks didn't see
a little girl in a chesterfield coat,
plaid bows on her five skimpy braids,
or stop me as I wept my way
toward the outside doors
and was spun through their transparency

Both poems are about incidents from the narrators' childhoods. "On the Spirit of Mildred Jordan" is about a more recent incident than "The Lost Daughter."

▶ out into the snow.

On the sidewalk Santa rang a shiny bell
and shifted from his right boot to his left
as the fingers in my mittens froze
and fell off, one by one.

"The Lost Daughter" seems to be more personal. I get a better feeling for the narrator's needs and wants from this poem.

▶ My skin, then my bones turned to stone
that parted the hurrying crowd,
until at last I drifted, thinned as the smoke
from an occasional pipe or cigarette,
through the thick white words people spoke.

Sometimes a taxi squealed its brakes
or beeped to pierce the solid, steady roar
of voices, wheels, and motors.
The same blue as the sky by now,
I rose like a float in the parade
I'd seen not long before:
a mouse tall as a department store
that nodded hugely as it moved
above our wonder down the avenue.

When Mama spat out my name
in fury and relief, I felt my face
fly back into focus. I formed again
instantaneously under her glaring eyes.
In the plate glass window I recognized
the shape Mama shook and embraced—
the runny nose, the eyes' frightened gleam,
the beret askew on hair gone wild—
and knew myself made whole again, her child.

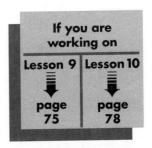

If you are
working on

Lesson 9	Lesson 10
⬇	⬇
page 75	page 78

In the 1960s and 1970s, Carole King was a very popular singer. One of her albums, *Tapestry*, was the best-selling album of the 1970s. The song below was included on that album. As well-liked as she was as a singer, King was even more popular among fellow musicians as a songwriter. Today King continues to write songs, tour, and produce albums.

You've Got a Friend

written and performed by Carole King

Write your own sidenotes in the margins comparing and contrasting the form and content of "You've Got a Friend" and "Por Mi Camino" on page 86.

When you're down and troubled
And you need some love and care
And nothing, nothing is going right
Close your eyes and think of me
And soon I will be there
To brighten up your darkest night

You just call out my name
And you know wherever I am
I'll come running to see you again
Winter, spring, summer or fall
All you have to do is call
And I'll be there
You've got a friend

If the sky above you
Grows dark and full of clouds
And that old north wind begins to blow
Keep your head together
And call my name out loud
Soon you'll hear me knocking at your door

You just call out my name
And you know wherever I am
I'll come running to see you again
Winter, spring, summer or fall
All you have to do is call
And I'll be there

Now ain't it good to know you've got a friend
When people can be so cold
They'll hurt you, and desert you
And take your soul if you let them
Oh, but don't you let them

You just call out my name
And you know wherever I am
I'll come running to see you again
Winter, spring, summer or fall
All you have to do is call
And I'll be there
You've got a friend

The Iguanas is a 1990s Tex-Mex group that performs songs in both English and Spanish. The five-member group got its start in New Orleans, where they were discovered by famous singer/songwriter Jimmy Buffett. The song below (written by Celso Piña) is a hit from their first big album, *The Iguanas*, produced in 1993.

Por Mi Camino (Along My Way)

Write your sidenotes here.

performed by The Iguanas

Along my way

In the evening as I am walking home
The firefly lights my way
And the song of the zenzontle says goodnight
To the sun that also lights my way

I look at the sky and I see the brilliant stars
Thinking of her, I console myself
But she is the cause of my sleepless nights
She is the cause of my sleepless nights

The moon rises pale and beautiful
Its reflection covers the horizon
And the stars that always accompany me
Remind me of her eyes
They remind me of her eyes

So I walk, always singing
The beautiful things I see pass by
Always looking on my way home
Along my way

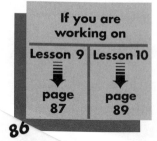

If you are working on

Lesson 9	Lesson 10
↓	↓
page 87	page 89

Reviewing Compare and Contrast

A. Read the songs "You've Got a Friend" and "Por Mi Camino (Along My Way)" on pages 84-86. Sing them to yourself if you know the tunes. When you have finished, use the Venn diagram below to compare and contrast the form and content of the two songs.

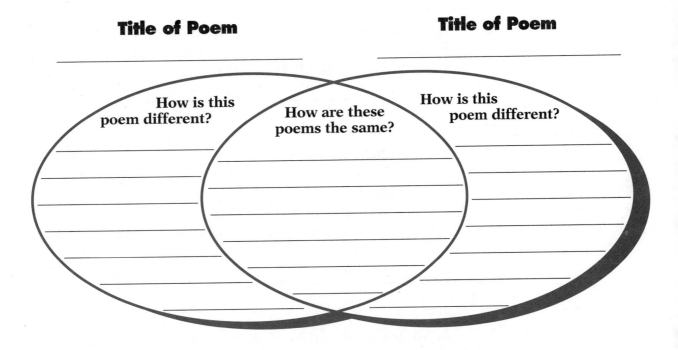

Title of Poem

Title of Poem

How is this poem different?

How are these poems the same?

How is this poem different?

B. How did comparing and contrasting the two songs help you better understand the meaning of the song lyrics? Write your ideas in a paragraph below.

Testing Compare and Contrast

A. In each pair of statements below, only one statement is true. Fill in the circle next to the true statement. Then on the lines provided, tell why you chose that statement.

1. ○ One way that "You've Got a Friend" and "Por Mi Camino (Along My Way)" are similar is that the speaker in both songs is a man.

   ○ One way that "You've Got a Friend" and "Por Mi Camino (Along My Way)" are similar is that they are both written in the first person.

   _____

   _____

2. ○ One difference between the songs is that "You've Got a Friend" has a chorus and "Por Mi Camino (Along My Way)" does not.

   ○ One difference between the songs is that "You've Got a Friend" has more than one verse and "Por Mi Camino (Along My Way)" does not.

   _____

   _____

3. ○ Another way that the songs are similar is that the singers of both songs are sad and lonely.

   ○ Another way that the songs are similar is that the singers of both songs are very concerned about another person.

   _____

   _____

B. Talk to a classmate about the songs. How do you feel about them? Which song do you like better? Compare and contrast your feelings about the songs to those of your classmate. Write your ideas below.

   _____

   _____

   _____

   _____

   _____

   _____

To begin
Lesson 10

↓

page
78

Reviewing Analogies

A. Reread the songs "You've Got a Friend" and "Por Mi Camino (Along My Way)." Then look at each group of five words below. Use the diagram to make an analogy using four of the words.

1. desert, north, fall, abandon, autumn

_____ : _____ : : _____ : _____

2. wind, clouds, call, blow, voice

_____ : _____ : : _____ : _____

3. horizon, aggravate, brilliant, lackluster, console

_____ : _____ : : _____ : _____

B. Think about the title of the song "Por Mi Camino (Along My Way)." What is the relationship of the phrase "my way" to the rest of the song? Use examples from the song in your response.

_____

_____

_____

_____

_____

_____

_____

_____

Testing Analogies

A. Read the pairs of analogies below and fill in the oval next to the analogy that is correct. Then use the first word in each analogy pair to fill in the blanks in the traditional English song that follows.

1. ○ discourteously : rudely :: just : wrong
   ○ discourteously : politely :: just : wrong
2. ○ heart : torso :: finger : hand
   ○ heart : torso :: writing : hand
3. ○ crave : yearn :: grant : deny
   ○ crave : yearn :: grant : give
4. ○ delight : neglect :: ready : available
   ○ delight : rapture :: ready : available

GREENSLEEVES

Alas! my love, you do me wrong
To cast me off _____,
And I have loved you so long,
Delighting in your company.

I have been ready at your hand
to grant whatever you would _____,
I have both waged life and land,
Your love and good will for to have.

Refrain: Greensleeves was all my joy,
*   Greensleeves was my _____,*
*   Greensleeves my _____ of gold,*
*   And who but my Lady Greensleeves*

B. Think about the words to one of your favorite songs. Then write an analogy using one or more of those words. First, write the analogy in sentence form below. Then use colons to write the analogy in the abbreviated style.

_____ : _____ :: _____ : _____

Unit SIX

BECOMING AN ACTIVE READER

Good readers are involved readers. When they read **poems**, they often look for a powerful message—or the main point the poet is making. To find the message, active readers respond to a poem's vivid language, imagery, and form.

Using Skills and Strategies

Identifying the main idea, or **subject of a poem,** will help you become an involved reader. You might ask: Are there certain words that describe the subject? Which phrases point to the subject? Which images reveal the subject of the poem?

Recognizing the poet's use of **figurative language** is another way to identify the subject. You might ask: Why is the poet using this simile or metaphor? How does personification reveal the message? Does the poet make a point by exaggerating?

In this unit, the skills of identifying the **subject of a poem** and analyzing **figurative language** will help you become an involved reader.

Reading the Poem

In poetry, thoughts, feelings, moods, and emotions are all expressed in a few words. Some poets use rhythm and repetition to convey the message in their poems. Other poets present their message through images and colorful descriptions in stanzas, or through various forms—numbered sections, indented lines, or words isolated in different parts of a line. Poets use these techniques to express their ideas.

Responding to Poems

Good readers respond to the rhythms, images, and words in poems. It is important to jot down your responses as you read the two poems in this unit, "The Power of Names" and "Housing Complex." Writing notes will help you remember your reactions to the poems. Refer to them when you discuss the poems with classmates.

Subject of a Poem

| *Lesson 11* | **Introducing** page 92 | **Practicing** page 93 | **Applying** page 94 | **Reviewing** page 102 | **Testing** page 103 |

Introducing Strategies

How do good readers discover the main idea, or **subject of a poem**? Like detectives, they study the lines of the poem, looking for details that give clues to the subject. Images in poems can create strong mental pictures that relate to the subject. Sometimes words and phrases are repeated and reveal what the poem is about. Other times, the subject is communicated in a line of the poem or in the title itself.

The diagram below shows how readers relate details of a poem to the subject.

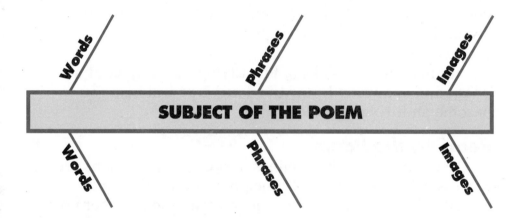

Reading the Poem

Read "The Power of Names" on pages 98-99 and the sidenotes on page 98. These notes show how one good reader discovered the subject of the poem. After you have finished reading, answer the questions below.

1. According to the reader, what may be the main idea or the subject of the poem?

_____

_____

2. Which words, phrases, and images does the reader notice as clues to the subject?

_____

_____

Practicing *Subject of a Poem*

A. Circle the letter next to the word or words that best complete each statement. Then on the line below each one, explain how this statement relates to the subject of "The Power of Names."

1. In the first stanza, the phrase that gives the BEST clue to the poem's meaning is

    a. "years number the times."   c. "and wonder if I will become like her."

    b. "I have worn her pain."

_____

2. The name *Pearl* in the poem refers to

    a. the poet.   b. a necklace.   c. the mother.

_____

3. In the third stanza, the image about swallowing something like a worm refers to

    a. hunger.   b. the mother's name.   c. a salmon.

_____

B. Explain in your own words what the poem is about. Use words from the poem to support your response.

_____

_____

_____

_____

_____

_____

_____

_____

_____

_____

_____

Applying *Subject of a Poem*

A. Read the words to the song below. Then answer the questions that follow it.

HE AIN'T HEAVY, HE'S MY BROTHER
by Bob Russell

The road is long, with many a winding turn,

that leads us to who knows where, who knows where.

But I'm strong, strong enough to carry him;

He Ain't Heavy, He's My Brother.

So on we go; his welfare is my concern.

No burden is he to bear, we'll get there.

For I know, he will not encumber me;

He Ain't Heavy, He's My Brother.

1. What is the message of this song?

_____

_____

2. What image helps reveal the message?

_____

_____

3. List some additional words that help the poet communicate his message.

_____

_____

B. Write an additional four-line stanza for this song. Make sure it reflects the message and format of the original poem.

_____

_____

_____

_____

_____

_____

To review

↓

page 102

Figurative Language

Lesson 12	Introducing page 95	Practicing page 96	Applying page 97	Reviewing page 104	Testing page 105

Introducing Strategies

Poets often use descriptive language, or **figurative language,** to express their feelings and ideas. Good readers of poetry look for such figures of speech, which may include:

- **simile,** comparing using *like* or *as: The baby was as good as gold.*
- **metaphor,** describing something as though it were something else: *My heart is a glass egg.*
- **personification**, giving human characteristics to objects or places: *The tree screamed with color.*
- **hyperbole,** exaggerating: *He tried a trillion times.*

The cluster below shows how a reader might identify and respond to figurative language in a poem.

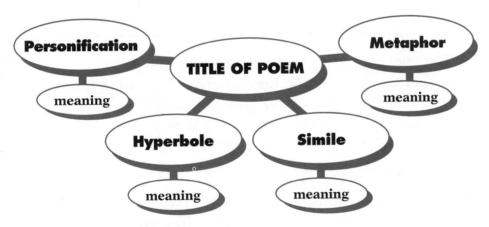

Reading the Poem

Reread the poem "The Power of Names" on pages 98-99. As you read, underline examples of figurative language. Then complete the items below.

1. Identify an example of figurative language in the poem.

_____

_____

2. What do you think this figure of speech means?

_____

_____

Practicing Figurative Language

A. Read the following statements about "The Power of Names" on pages 98-99. Circle the letter in front of the word or words that best complete each statement. Then on the lines provided, tell why you made each choice.

1. The poet compares slipping on a glove to
   a. dressing in her mother's clothes.
   b. taking on her mother's name.
   c. becoming something nonliving.
   d. acting formally rather than informally.

   _____

2. The figure of speech in the line "Her name, at times, does not fit me," is an example of
   a. simile.
   b. metaphor.
   c. personification.
   d. hyperbole.

   _____

3. The poet compares herself to a salmon to show
   a. that she cannot stop her pattern of returning home.
   b. that she cannot survive going upstream.
   c. that she cannot survive in deep water.
   d. why the poet says her mother's name.

   _____

B. Choose an example of figurative language from the poem. Explain why you think it is effective in communicating the subject, or main idea, of the poem.

_____

_____

_____

_____

_____

_____

_____

_____

Applying *Figurative Language*

A. Read the poem below. Then answer the questions that follow it.

MY HEART

My heart is a boat,

riding waves, each a million feet high.

Do you question my sincerity?

Truth is like salt,

it stings, it stings.

The largest grain of salt in the highest wave

laughs like a soprano as I glide over it.

Do you question my sincerity?

My heart is a boat,

coming near you, then going far away.

1. What is an example of a simile or metaphor in this poem?

_____

_____

2. How does the simile or metaphor you chose for #1 help communicate the meaning of the poem?

_____

_____

3. What is an example of personification or hyperbole in this poem?

_____

_____

4. How does the example you chose in #3 help communicate the meaning of the poem?

_____

_____

B. Imagine that you are the poet who wrote "My Heart," and you want to add a line of figurative language to the poem. Write that line below. Use your imagination.

_____

To review

↓

page 104

The poem below comes from Irma McClaurin's third book, *Pearl's Song*. She is also working on a biography of African American writer James Baldwin, part of which was published in a book titled *Black Writers Redefine the Struggle*. Currently, McClaurin teaches at the University of Massachusetts in Amherst, where she is working on a Ph.D. in anthropology.

I think the word *Power* is a clue to what the poet is saying in the poem about names.

The notes in the margin show how one good reader looked for images, words, and phrases as clues to the subject of the poem.
In the first line she compares having a name to wearing a glove—a glove protects but it also hides what's inside.

Maybe the main point the poet is making is really a question— how similar are we to those closest to us? Her mother's life, she says, is a second skin.

Continue to look closely for details in the poem that may be clues to the subject, or main point, of the poem. Ask yourself as you read, *What do these clues tell me about the power of names?* Write your notes in the margins.

The Power of Names

by Irma McClaurin

▶ I slip my mother's name on like a glove
and wonder if I will become like her
absolutely.
Years number the times I have worn her pain
as a child, as a teenager, as a woman—my second skin—
or screamed her screams
as she sat, silver head bowed
silent
▶ hedging the storm.

Her name, at times, does not fit me.
I take it, turn it over on my tongue—
a key.
Shape my lips around its vowels
hoping to unlock elusive doors,
understand the instincts
my body follows.
The family named her Pearl,
a first among them;

yet others have owned this name.
They haunt me.
I follow their destiny.

Each year I return home,
a salmon caught in an act of survival.
I search my mother's face
neatly carved in obsidian
and wonder
how much of myself I owe this woman
whose name I have swallowed like a worm.
Her inner soul transferred through the eating.

I slip my mother's name on
with wonder
and become like her
absolutely.

If you are
working on

Lesson 11 | Lesson 12

page 92 | page 95

Isabel Fraire, born in Mexico City in 1934, learned English from her Canadian grandmother. Fraire has this to say about writing poetry: "My only reason for writing is to grasp [a] moment of awareness and somehow leave it there, outside me, in readiness for any who wish to share it." The poem below was translated from Spanish by Thomas Hoeksema.

Housing Complex

by Isabel Fraire

As you read, take notes about details that are clues to the subject of the poem "Housing Complex." You may also want to underline examples of figurative language.

I.

morning rises slowly like a mist climbing
        and spreading through the air

a child crosses   squares of green grass
    running   jumping   running
      carrying
          a shopping bag in its hand

II.

the apartment buildings
        present flat rectangular   surfaces

    the windows are equipped with gray steel shutters
        that close   or open
           like lids
              each room a box

the garden   of smooth green grass   like a new carpet
    is framed by regular rows of identical trees
        that cast an oblong shadow
          like a wall

III.

no one speaks to each other here   a neighbor tells me
       breaking the rule
             after a year
at predetermined hours
            two or three old men and a child
          take their respective dogs out for a walk
        one of them is in the habit of
               letting the dog run loose
       the others stop
          each time
              the dog stops

IV.

usually silence prevails
             broken only by the noise of traffic
     that swells
       at the hours when offices open or close

but occasionally
     through paper-thin walls   one overhears
       a bitter violent   discussion
          full of resentment
        for a ruined life
      melodramatic panting
           background music
      from the television set

V.

a block away
    large bulldozers
      busily demolish a small grove

in order to erect a mass of buildings
    exactly like this one

If you are
working on

Lesson 11	Lesson 12
⬇	⬇
page 102	page 104

Reviewing *Subject of a Poem*

A. Read "Housing Complex" on pages 100-101. As you read, take some notes about the words, phrases, and images that are clues to the subject of the poem. Use the diagram below to organize your notes.

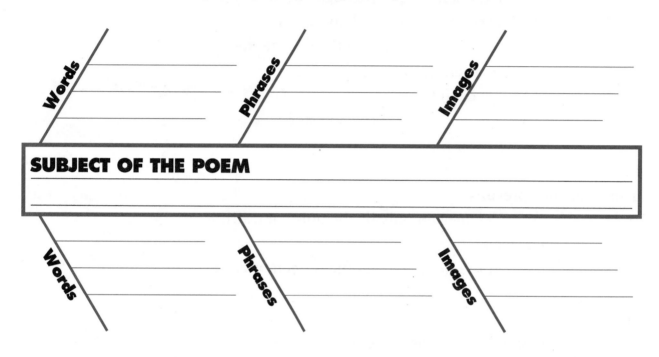

Words **Phrases** **Images**

SUBJECT OF THE POEM

Words **Phrases** **Images**

B. Write a paragraph that summarizes in your own words how the poet feels about the housing complex. Use details from the poem to support your ideas.

_____

_____

_____

_____

_____

_____

_____

_____

_____

_____

_____

_____

Testing *Subject of a Poem*

A. Each statement below about "Housing Complex" is incorrect. Rewrite each one so that it accurately reflects the main idea, or subject, of the poem.

1. This poem expresses the poet's positive feelings about large city buildings and the people who live in them.

_____

_____

2. The poet is basically optimistic that the buildings and city life will greatly improve.

_____

_____

3. The things the poet likes most about the housing complex are its interesting design and the friendliness of its people.

_____

_____

B. Create another image that expresses the poet's feelings about the housing complex. You may wish to develop the image into a sixth stanza.

_____

_____

_____

_____

_____

_____

_____

_____

_____

_____

_____

To begin
Lesson 12

page
95

Reviewing *Figurative Language*

A. Reread "Housing Complex" on pages 100-101. Underline any examples of figurative language you find, including similes, metaphors, personification, or hyperbole. Then think about the meaning of each figure of speech you underlined as you complete the cluster below.

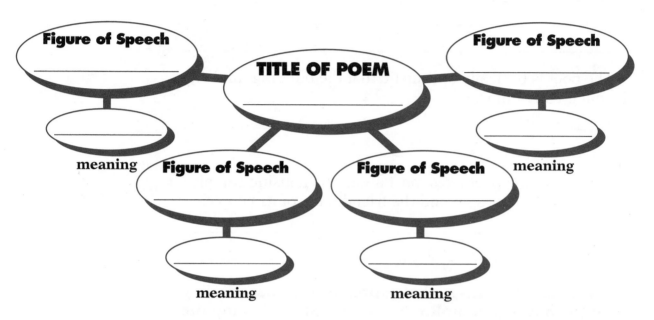

B. Think about a place where you would like to live. Describe the place by using comparisons or exaggerations and by giving nonhuman subjects human traits.

_____

_____

_____

_____

_____

_____

_____

_____

_____

_____

_____

Testing *Figurative Language*

A. Each pair of lines below is from the poem "Housing Complex" on pages 100-101. Mark an X next to the line that represents an example of figurative language. Then, on the lines provided, identify the figure of speech.

_____   morning rises like a mist climbing

_____   a child crosses   squares of green grass

_____

_____   the garden   of smooth green grass   like a new carpet

_____   no one speaks to each other here   a neighbor tells me

_____

_____   gray steel shutters   that close   or open like lids

_____   through paper-thin walls   one overhears

_____

B. Which example of figurative language in the poem do you particularly like? What about it do you like? How does it help communicate the meaning of the poem to you?

_____
_____
_____
_____
_____
_____
_____
_____
_____
_____
_____

Unit SEVEN

BECOMING AN ACTIVE READER

Good readers are strategic readers. As they read **reference articles**, they keep their purposes for reading in mind. They ask questions and form opinions about the facts and ideas presented in the articles.

Using Skills and Strategies

Asking questions about the topic will help you understand the material when you read a **reference article**. You might ask: What do I already know about the topic? What do I hope to find out by reading it? How can I tell what is presented on the topic?

Understanding the **technical terms** a writer uses is a key to understanding a reference article. When you come across a technical term, you might ask: Do I know what this term means? How does the term relate to *this* subject?

In this unit, **reading a reference article** by questioning and identifying **key words** will help you read strategically.

Reading the Reference Article

People from many cultures have made contributions to the arts, the sciences, and the government of our country. Many reference sources are available in libraries that focus on people from all groups who have excelled in specific areas. These books provide quick ways to obtain in-depth information on a subject. Ask your librarian for reference sources with articles about people or groups that interest you.

Responding to Reference Articles

Good readers respond to reference articles by noting new information and relating it to what they already know. It is important to jot down your thoughts as you read the reference articles in this unit, "The Dance Theatre of Harlem" and "Maria Tallchief: America's Prima Ballerina." Use these notes to discuss the articles.

Reading a Reference Article

| Lesson 13 | Introducing page 107 | Practicing page 108 | Applying page 109 | Reviewing page 122 | Testing page 123 |

Introducing *Strategies*

Good readers know they will often find articles on related topics in a reference source. Longer reference articles contain detailed information on a topic, organized under subheadings. Before reading the articles, good readers think about what they already know about the topic. They ask themselves what they want to find out. Then they skim the introduction, the subheadings, and the closing paragraphs. As they read, they keep notes on what they learn.

The chart below shows the questions good readers ask themselves as they **read a reference article**.

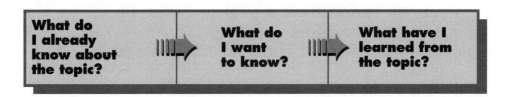

Reading a Reference Article

Read the reference article "The Dance Theater of Harlem" on pages 113-117 and the sidenotes on pages 113-114. These notes show how one good reader asked questions and responded to the information in the article. After reading, answer the questions below.

1. Before reading the article, how did the reader know what kind of information the article contained?

_____

_____

_____

2. What are some of the things the reader wanted to find out about the Dance Theater of Harlem?

_____

_____

_____

Practicing **Reading a Reference Article**

A. The items below are based on the reference article "The Dance Theater of Harlem." Circle the letter next to the words that best complete each statement. On the lines provided, explain why you selected that answer.

1. The purpose of the first two paragraphs in the article is to

    a. provide audience attendance statistics for DTH.

    b. introduce the topic to be covered.

    c. give background about Arthur Mitchell.

    d. provide quotes by community leaders.

_____

_____

2. To find out if the article includes information that the reader wants to know, the reader should

    a. read the entire article, then skim the headings.

    b. read the sections one at a time.

    c. skim the introduction, the subheadings, and any pictures.

    d. none of the above.

_____

_____

3. After skimming, the reader would know NOT to refer to this article for information about

    a. the first African American ballet dancers.

    b. important dates in the history of DTH.

    c. the prejudice African American dancers have had to confront.

    d. entrance requirements for DTH's dance classes.

_____

_____

B. Imagine that your community is preparing an information book for new residents. You have been asked to write a brief article about your school. List the subheadings you would include in your article.

_____

_____

_____

Applying *Reading a Reference Article*

Read the title and subtitle of the opening paragraph of a reference article below. Then complete items 1 and 2 *before* you read the paragraph itself. After you have finished reading, complete item 3.

1. List some of the things you already know about music and ballet.

_____

_____

_____

2. List some questions you have about ballet and its music. What would you like to know?

_____

_____

_____

WHEN BALLET MUSIC PLAYED A SMALL PART

In its beginning, ballet was not a separate, full-length performance as we know it today. Music played a small part. Ballets were usually small dances in the middle of a play. The play often featured music that already existed. Ballet music, even when written by well-known composers such as Mozart and Beethoven, was not the featured part of a performance. Up to the end of the 1800s, ballet music was uninteresting. One piece seemed very much like another. Then, at the end of the nineteenth century and early into the twentieth century, ballet music changed dramatically. Its music, once relatively unimportant, became a major influence on the art of dance.

3. What did you learn by reading this paragraph?

_____

_____

_____

_____

_____

_____

To review

⬇

page 122

Key Words

Lesson 14	Introducing *page 110*	Practicing *page 111*	Applying *page 112*	Reviewing *page 124*	Testing *page 125*

Introducing Strategies

To read informational articles effectively, good readers look for and identify **key words.** Key words may be technical terms that are specific to the subject. For example, key words in an article about organic gardening might be *mulch* or *compost pile.* Sometimes they are printed in dark or italic type. After identifying a key word, a good reader will stop and ask questions such as: *How is this word important to the topic of the article? Is this word related to a word I already know?* Identifying key words and relating them to words you already know will help you read with greater understanding.

The chart below shows how readers identify words they already know that may be related to the key words.

Reading the Reference Article

Reread the reference article "The Dance Theater of Harlem." As you read, underline some key words. After reading, answer the questions below.

1. What words did you identify as key words? List several.

_____

_____

_____

2. Which of these words are technical terms? What words do you already know that may be related?

_____

_____

_____

Practicing Key Words

A. Read each sentence and circle any key words. Then on the line below each sentence, write any words you know that are related to the key word or words.

1. Naurice Roberts performed with a ballet troupe at the Civic Opera House in Chicago.

_____

2. Mitchell became a *principal* in the New York City Ballet.

_____

3. Beginning students were taught *barre* exercises.

_____

4. More advanced students learned complex techniques such as the straight-legged *arabesque*.

_____

5. Katherine Dunham, the African American dancer and choreographer, received her training in Chicago.

_____

6. Janet Collins was the *prima ballerina* at the Metropolitan Opera House.

_____

B. Describe an activity in which you regularly participate, such as a sport, musical group, or hobby. Include terms that are specific to your subject, or words that readers might identify as key words.

_____

_____

_____

_____

_____

_____

_____

_____

Applying Key Words

Read the article below. As you read, circle the key words you identify. Then complete the items that follow.

"WRITING" A DANCE

How can you preserve a dance on paper so that dancers can "read" it, so someone, another time, can perform it? You can "write" a dance by using a system called dance notation.

Until the first system of dance notation was developed by Rudolf Laban in the 1920s, choreographers relied on memory. Dances were taught and passed along by demonstration. Laban's method, called Labanotation, uses symbols to show the position of the legs. Symbols also indicate speed and direction, so choreographers can describe every aspect of every movement. Other notation systems are used as well now, and most dances are also recorded on film.

1. Write the words you identified as key words.

_____

_____

_____

_____

2. Which of the key words you identified are technical words, specific only to this subject? Explain how you made your choice.

_____

_____

_____

_____

3. List three key words that remind you of words or terms you already know. Explain how they are related.

_____

_____

_____

_____

To review ↓ page 124

As a child in the 1960s, Naurice Roberts performed with a ballet troupe at the Civic Opera House in Chicago. In her own way, Roberts helped to introduce African Americans into the world of ballet. In this article, she discusses the development of African American ballet in the United States and the key role played by Arthur Mitchell, founder of the Dance Theater of Harlem.

The Dance Theater of Harlem

by Naurice Roberts

The Dance Theater of Harlem (DTH) is a well-known and highly respected arts institution. It includes a fully accredited school, a ballet company, and a full range of educational and social programs. DTH is located in New York City's Harlem community. It is considered to be the top African American ballet company in the United States.

Since its beginning, DTH has challenged the stereotyping and prejudice that led to a lack of African American performers in the dance world. It has also helped African Americans meet the challenge of performing classical ballet.

The First African American Ballet Dancers

Helena Just-De Arms was the first African American to be formally trained in classical ballet. Born in 1900, she was only 4 years old when her parents, who worked in vaudeville, took her abroad. She studied ballet in Brussels, Belgium, and became the "dancing baby" in her parents' touring musical act.

In the 1930s, African Americans managed to receive training by Russian and other ballet teachers who emigrated to the United States. Usually, these teachers were not prejudiced against African Americans. Still, they had to offer private lessons or small, separate classes to African Americans to avoid criticism from those who were prejudiced. Katherine Dunham, the celebrated African American dancer and choreographer, received her training in Chicago in this "secret" way.

In 1938, Mary Bruce helped to break the silence surrounding African Americans in ballet. She developed a comprehensive dance program for African Americans in Harlem. Her school presented "starbuds" recitals, often at Carnegie Hall, that featured African American dancers.

Since I'm looking for information about ballet in the United States I wonder if this article will help. I'll skim the subheadings to find out what information is included.

The notes in the margins show one reader's thoughts while reading a reference article. Notice how they reflect what the reader already knew, hopes to find out, and learned.

I wondered who the first African American ballet dancers were and where they danced. I'll learn that here.

Other African American ballet pioneers included Doris Jones and Claire Haywood. Both dancers and teachers, they opened a school in Washington, D.C. Similarly, Essie Marie Dorsey taught the art of ballet to numerous African American students in Baltimore and Philadelphia from the 1920s until World War II.

▶ Early African American Ballet Companies

People have been prejudiced against African Americans. I wonder if the early ballet companies were successful.

A number of African American classical ballet companies were formed after World War II. Most were unsuccessful. Generally, they suffered from the same problems that affected many small ballet companies: a lack of money, inadequate training, and limited audiences. However, the African American companies also had to deal with the additional problems stemming from racism.

Ballet Becomes Integrated

Until the 1950s, few African Americans performed classical ballet. Finally, in 1951, Janet Collins became the first African American ballerina to perform at New York City's Metropolitan Opera House. She was the star of the show, the *prima* ballerina. To gain recognition, however, Collins had to start her career in Broadway musicals. She achieved fame there when she won the Donaldson Award for Best Dancer in a Broadway Musical. Only after

Oh, I see that some dancers entered the ballet world from other areas of dance.

▶ receiving this prestigious award was she accepted into the world of classical dance.

The other African American trailblazer in classical dance was Arthur Mitchell. In 1955, he became the first African American to solo in the New York City Ballet. He was also the first African American to permanently join a ballet company.

Mitchell danced superbly. He quickly became a *principal* in the New York City Ballet. Although he was able to perform throughout the world, discrimination limited his opportunities in the United States. He was still the New York City Ballet's only African American dancer when he left the company in 1966. He then performed on

Arthur Mitchell must have been quite a dancer! Not only was he the first African American to solo in the New York City Ballet but he also performed on Broadway and served as an artistic director.

▶ Broadway and served as artistic director for Broadway dance shows.

The Beginnings of the Dance Theater of Harlem

Arthur Mitchell was born in Harlem in 1934. He began formal ballet training there in his late teens. In 1969, Mitchell returned to Harlem. He had been greatly upset by the assassination of Dr. Martin Luther King, Jr., in 1968, and was determined to help young African

Americans. Mitchell wanted to provide them with cultural opportunities and experiences. He and Karel Shook, an excellent teacher and choreographer who was his mentor, formed the Dance Theater of Harlem in 1969.

The DTH began as a school. Its purpose was to teach young African Americans about the art of dance—classical ballet, modern dance, and African American traditional dance. By doing so, Mitchell hoped to build self-esteem and pride in his students. The long-term goal of the DTH was to develop a performing dance company.

The DTH began with only two teachers and 30 students. Beginning students were taught *barre* exercises, while more advanced students learned more complex techniques, including raised-leg poses, such as the straight-legged *arabesques* and bent-knee *attitudes*. The school was housed in a Harlem church basement. However, with financial aid from the Ford Foundation, it expanded rapidly. Talented, well-known dancers came to the DTH to teach, which led to a huge increase in student enrollment. Soon, hopeful young dancers came to the DTH from all over the world.

Write your own sidenotes as you continue reading the article. Focus on what you already know, what you want to know, and what you have learned.

The goal of creating a dance company became a reality in 1971. The DTH ballet company's debut performance was at New York City's Guggenheim Museum. Words such as "highly professional" and "engaging" were used by dance critics to describe the performance. *The New York Times* praised the school as "one of ballet's most exciting undertakings." Under the artistic direction of Arthur Mitchell, the dance company had a uniquely American flavor. After all, it had been born and developed in New York City.

DTH on Tour in the 1970s

Ballet companies, like other entertainment groups, go on tour so that more people will become aware of them. The Dance Theater of Harlem was no different. Although it quickly became a sensation in New York City, it wanted to broaden its audience. During the 1970s, it gave sold-out performances throughout the United States, Europe, Mexico, the British Isles, and the Caribbean.

As the company's reputation grew, it received many invitations. During the Reagan administration, the President and First Lady praised the company for its opening performance at the Kennedy Center in Washington, D.C. They then invited the DTH to perform at President Reagan's first state dinner. This dinner honored the official visit of Great Britain's Prime Minister, Margaret Thatcher.

The DTH was also asked to give command performances for European royalty. For example, the King of Norway and the Queen of England both extended invitations.

In Demand in the 1980s and 1990s

Arthur Mitchell and the full company have been showcased in major newspaper and magazine articles. They have been featured in numerous television programs, including *60 Minutes* and a prime-time ABC News Special hosted by Peter Jennings. The DTH was also selected to participate in the closing ceremonies of the 1984 Olympic Games. In addition, the U.S. Post Office selected the company to appear on one of a series of stamps honoring dance.

In 1988, the DTH was the first ballet company invited by the U.S. Information Agency to perform in the Soviet Union. Their historic five-week tour was enthusiastically received by Soviet audiences. The most talked-about performance on the tour was a sold-out show at the

Kirov Theater. The DTH received a rare standing ovation that night.

At its first appearance in Africa, in 1992, the DTH performed at the National Culture Center in Cairo, Egypt. Later that year the company performed to sold-out, integrated audiences in South Africa. Because of its concern with the results of racial segregation in that country, the DTH included community outreach and educational programs as part of its tour. The DTH remains committed to its first and most vital mission: to provide cultural opportunities to disadvantaged young people.

The Dance Theater of Harlem Makes a Difference

With 500 dancers enrolled each semester, the DTH has trained thousands of young people. Many have gone on to excel in the performing arts. Others have become successful educators, business people, and industry leaders. Most will say that they were inspired by their experiences with the DTH.

Because of the work of Arthur Mitchell, African Americans have been able to enter a new field. Because of his challenge, the world of dance will never be the same. The transformation continues, and the DTH remains one of the strongest forces behind it.

If you are
working on

Lesson 13 | Lesson 14

page
107

page
110

Susan Arkeketa, an Otoe-Creek teacher and writer, grew up in Tulsa, Oklahoma. She began ballet lessons as a child because she admired the Tallchief sisters, Maria and Marjorie. From 1978 to 1980, the author was selected to serve as Miss Indian America, becoming in her own way a role model for young Native Americans.

Maria Tallchief: America's Prima Ballerina

by Susan Arkeketa

Maria Tallchief decided to become a professional dancer when she was 15 years old. Her determination led her to become one of the world's greatest ballerinas. During her long career, she performed in many of the world's leading dance companies, including the New York City Ballet Company and the Ballet Russe de Monte Carlo.

Early Childhood—Nurturing a Talent

Maria was born in Fairfax, Oklahoma, on January 24, 1925. Her father, Alexander Tallchief, was an Osage; his father had served as chief of the Osage Nation. Her mother, Ruth Porter Tallchief, was of Scotch-Irish descent. Maria's birth name is Elizabeth Marie Tallchief. In Fairfax, everyone called her Betty Marie.

Betty Marie started dance lessons at the age of 4. By the time she was 5, Betty Marie was dancing regularly for audiences in the area. Her sister Marjorie soon joined her in the dance acts. Both girls also excelled at the piano.

Ruth Tallchief knew that her daughters had special gifts. She wanted to provide more music and dance lessons for them. Eventually, the family moved to Los Angeles, where the girls' talents could be nurtured.

When Betty Marie was 8, she and Marjorie started taking ballet lessons from Ernest Belcher. Belcher disagreed with the girls' former training. He told the girls that they would have to learn ballet from the beginning.

Belcher worked the sisters hard, teaching them ballet history, techniques, and fundamentals. Betty Marie learned how to warm up at the *bar*, do *port de bras* (five positions), *plies* (knee bends), and *enchainments* (combinations of steps). She began to be noticed for her exceptional dance ability. Belcher himself acknowledged

As you read, use the margins to note things you already know, what you want to know more about, and what you have learned.

her talents when he asked her to dance in the *corps de ballet* at the Los Angeles Civic Opera House.

In Betty Marie's first year of high school, Belcher informed her that she needed more advanced training than he could offer. He sent her to study under Madame Bronislava Nijinska. Under Madame Nijinska, Betty Marie practiced ever more complex moves.

In 1941, Madame Nijinska took Betty Marie to see the Ballet Russe de Monte Carlo, a highly regarded troupe. After the performance, Betty Marie went backstage to meet the dancers, including the prima ballerina Alexandra Danilova. She also met Serge Denhan, the director of the Ballet Russe de Monte Carlo, and performed a solo for him. When she finished, he told her, "You look as if you may some day make Ballet Russe material." Betty Marie kept those words in her heart and worked toward that goal.

Ballet Russe de Monte Carlo—The Start of a Career

Betty Marie's dream came true in 1942, when she joined the Ballet Russe as the 17-year-old protégée of Bronislava Nijinska. While with that company, Betty Marie changed her name to Maria Tallchief. She also met the famous choreographer George Balanchine. He decided to help her develop a dance style and philosophy. At that time, dancers whom Balanchine selected were destined for fame.

Under Balanchine's direction Betty Marie worked hard to perfect her classical movements—the *pointe* and *fouettes,* for example. She was a strong dancer and did magnificent leaps and twirls.

In February 1945, Balanchine offered Maria a corps role in a dance. She danced so well that Balanchine gave her a part in his production of the *Ballet Imperial.* It was the start of a long working relationship.

Balanchine soon offered Maria a chance to show her growing ability, in the production of *Le Baiser de la Fee.* Balanchine wanted Maria to dance the part of the Fee, a very difficult role. This role requires a dancer to assume three different personalities: the Ice Maiden, the Gypsy Fortune Teller, and the Bride. In dancing the role, Maria demonstrated that she was indeed a great talent. The critics declared her a "ballerina born on stage."

Soon afterwards, Maria married Balanchine. The two worked together as husband and wife for several years. Maria eventually left the Ballet Russe and joined her husband's company, the Ballet Society. The company later changed its name to the New York City Ballet Company.

The Firebird—Maria Becomes a Star

On November 27, 1949, the New York City Ballet Company presented *The Firebird*. Maria danced the extremely difficult role of the firebird in all its grace and glory. Critics and audiences loved her performance. Each *Firebird* performance sold out.

When the season ended, the American Ballet Theater asked her to join the company as guest prima ballerina. Marie did her tour with the American Ballet Theater and then returned to the New York City Ballet Company.

Eventually, Balanchine and Maria decided to end their marriage. However, they continued working as dance partners. Balanchine created dozens of roles for Maria over the years. Together, they brought fame to the New York City Ballet Company.

In April 1956, Maria married Henry D. Paschen, Jr., and they had one daughter—Elise Maria. Soon afterwards, Maria returned to New York and her successful career.

The Significance of Her Career

The New York City Ballet Company, with Maria as its star, launched the era of American ballet. Maria Tallchief danced throughout the world. Wherever she went, she symbolized everything grand about American ballet. Along the way, Tallchief received many honors and awards. One of her favorite honors was a name—the Native American name Wa-Xthe-Thonbe ("Princess of Two Standards"), which was given to her by the Osage Nation. Another was the designation of Maria Tallchief Day, June 29, 1953, an honor given to her by the Oklahoma State Senate.

Maria's long hard hours and determination made her a ballet legend. In April 1966, she decided to "hang up her shoes" and become a full-time mother and wife. She said that "marriage and dancing are both very important, but it is better to take them one at a time."

Maria still had one very important performance, however. On October 28, 1967, Maria and her sister Marjorie, along with Native American ballerinas Yvonne Chouteau, Rosella Hightower, and Mosscelyn Larkin, performed *The Four Moons*. This ballet was written especially for the Native American ballerinas from Oklahoma.

The Chicago City Ballet—Continued Importance

Ballet continues to flow in Maria's veins. She has never cut her ties with the dance world. In fact, quite the opposite is true. Since "retiring" from ballet, Maria Tallchief has created one of the world's finest ballet companies, the Chicago City Ballet. The company's first season began in June 1981, with Maria serving as artistic director and her sister Marjorie as school director. Since then, the company has produced many successful performances, becoming world famous. It seems Maria will continue to live up to her Native American family name, KiHiKahStah (Tallchief) in the world of ballet.

If you are working on

Lesson 13	Lesson 14
page 122	page 124

Reviewing *Reading a Reference Article*

A. Read the article "Maria Tallchief: America's Prima Ballerina" on pages 118-121. Before you read, skim the article and write some questions about what you want to find out. Make notes while reading about what you learn. When you have finished, use the sidenotes you wrote to fill in the chart below.

What do I already know about Maria Tallchief?	What do I want to know?	What have I learned from the article?

B. Think about an interest you have in the arts or in sports, for example. Write four subheadings for an article on the topic. Then on a separate sheet of paper, write an opening paragraph and a closing paragraph for the article.

_____

_____

_____

_____

_____

_____

_____

_____

_____

Testing Reading a Reference Article

A. The statements below are based on the article "Maria Tallchief: America's Prima Ballerina." Read each statement. Write T in the space next to each statement that is true. Write F if the statement is false.

_____ **1.** By reading the opening paragraphs of the article, a reader can learn how Maria Tallchief's Native American heritage has influenced her dancing.

_____ **2.** To find out the highlights of the article, a reader could first skim the subheadings.

_____ **3.** One purpose of the article is to inform readers about Native American Dance.

_____ **4.** A reader would look under the subheading "The Significance of Her Career" to find out why Maria Tallchief founded the Chicago City Ballet.

_____ **5.** One purpose of this article is to describe the important contributions Balanchine has made to ballet.

_____ **6.** To understand this article, a reader would have to know complicated ballet terms.

_____ **7.** To learn how dances are designed, a reader would look for reference material on choreography.

B. Think about a topic you are interested in learning more about. Write five questions about the topic. Then find the title of a specific reference source that would help you find the answers. Ask your school or local librarian for assistance.

_____

_____

_____

_____

_____

_____

_____

_____

_____

_____

To begin
Lesson 14

page
110

Reviewing *Key Words*

A. Reread the article about Maria Tallchief on pages 118-121. As you read, circle the key words you identify. Use these words to complete the chart below.

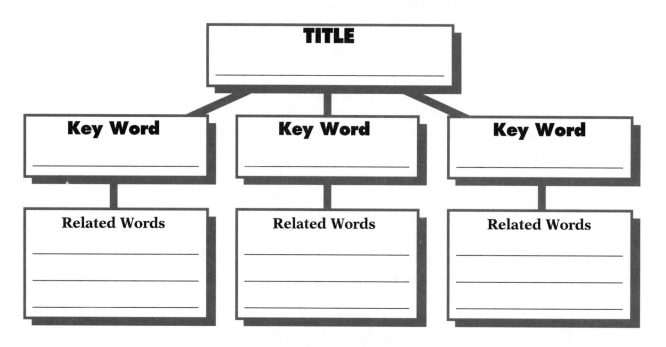

B. Many young dancers have looked toward Maria Tallchief as a role model. Describe someone whom you consider to be a role model. Give at least three reasons you have chosen this person.

_____

_____

_____

_____

_____

_____

_____

_____

_____

_____

_____

Testing Key Words

A. Read the paragraphs below. Then read both paragraphs a second time and choose a word from the following list to complete each sentence.

ballet master   barre   corps de ballet
movements   prima ballerina troupe

Tess found, after she had read an article about ballet, that her notes were scrambled. Actually, she hadn't taken very good notes at all, and now she tried to remember what some of the terms meant. The principal female dancer, she knew, was the _____.

That was easy because the term reminded her of a word she knew that meant "first." *Point* and *fouettes* were classical ballet dance _____, they were not practice exercises. The dancers did exercises at the _____.

The _____ was not a military dance; it referred to the dancers who performed as a group, not as solo dancers. Tess figured that out because she knew the word _____ was another word for *company* when referring to all the dancers together. This organization of dancers, was under the charge of the _____, who was responsible for the training and rehearsals of the dancers.

B. Choose a topic you are interested in studying. Read at least two reference articles on the topic. List, below, several key words you found in the article. Then, on a separate sheet of paper, write a paragraph summarizing what you have learned. Use the key words in your summary.

_____

_____

Unit EIGHT

BECOMING AN ACTIVE READER

Good readers are strategic readers. They approach **encyclopedia articles** with a plan in mind. They form opinions based on sound judgment. Good readers read articles purposefully.

Using Skills and Strategies

Making judgments will help you understand the information in the articles you read. You might ask: How does this compare to something the writer said earlier? In what ways is this idea different from or similar to what I already know? What does this information tell me?

Visual aids such as maps, graphs, tables, and charts can help you locate information quickly in an article. You might ask: What do I need to find out? Which visual aid will help me? What key words can I look for?

In this unit, the skills **making judgments** and using **visual aids** will help you read strategically.

Reading the Encyclopedia Article

Encyclopedias contain a great deal of information about thousands of subjects. When you read an encyclopedia article, you may feel overwhelmed by the amount of information presented. Take your time as you read. Stop and ask questions. Go back and reread sections a second, even a third, time. Take notes. Then summarize what you have learned.

Responding to Encyclopedia Articles

Good readers respond to encyclopedia entries by developing a new awareness of the subject. As you read the entries "Hong Kong" and "Venezuela" write your own questions and comments in the side margins. Writing these sidenotes will help you remember the material you've read. Refer to them when you discuss the entries with your classmates.

Making Judgments

| Lesson 15 | Introducing page 127 | Practicing page 128 | Applying page 129 | Reviewing page 144 | Testing page 145 |

Introducing Strategies

Good readers **make judgments** based on the information given in encyclopedia articles. To do this, they identify topics, or information, covered in the articles. Then they make comparisons, or identify similarities in the information. They also contrast the information by finding differences. Comparing and contrasting information will help you form opinions and make judgments.

Use a chart like the one below to help you compare and contrast information. The information on the chart shows how one good reader compared specific information while reading about China and Hong Kong.

	CHINA	HONG KONG
Population	1,165,888,000	5,799,000
Economics	agricultural; average earnings: $370/yr	business related; average earnings: $12,500/yr
Politics	communist; much government influence	colonial government; little government influence
Culture	less Western influence	much Western influence

Reading the Encyclopedia Article

Read the article "Hong Kong" and the sidenotes on pages 133-137. These notes show how one good reader noted similarities and differences between the island colony of Hong Kong and mainland China. After reading, complete the items below.

1. Write three differences the reader found between China and Hong Kong.

_____

_____

2. What did the reader learn about the geography of Hong Kong and China? In the 1980s, how did this affect their relationship?

_____

_____

Practicing Making Judgments

A. The incomplete statements below are based on the article "Hong Kong." Circle the letter in front of the word or words that best complete each statement. On the lines provided make a judgment based on the facts from the article that support your answer.

1. The populations of China and Hong Kong are alike in that both are predominantly _____.

    a. male   c. young

    b. female   d. Chinese

_____

_____

2. Wages and salaries in China are _____ they are in Hong Kong.

    a. much lower than   c. about half of what

    b. much higher than   d. the same as

_____

_____

3. In China the government has a great influence over the people; in Hong Kong _____.

    a. there is no government

    b. the government also enjoys great control

    c. the people feel little influence from the government

    d. the people are struggling to change the government

_____

_____

B. Identify two major differences between Hong Kong and China. Make a judgement about how you think they will affect the takeover of Hong Kong by China in 1997.

_____

_____

_____

_____

_____

_____

Applying *Making Judgments*

Read the following paragraph. Then complete the items that follow.

MACAO: ANOTHER PIECE OF CHINA

On a map, Macao looks to be part of China and is considered by many of its residents to be part of China. It's actually a Portuguese territory made up of the city of Macao on the mainland and three islands in the mouth of the Zhu Jiang. Although a governor appointed by the president of Portugal and an assembly govern Macao, the Chinese government can veto any laws they make. China will gain full control in December 1999, two and a half years after regaining control of Hong Kong, which now has no direct governmental ties with China.

Like Hong Kong, most of the residents of Macao are Chinese; most of the rest, however, are Portuguese. They are employed in tourist-related jobs and in industry. As in Hong Kong, there is little agriculture. Macao buys most of its food and water from China.

1. What is the subject of the article? _____

2. To what is it being compared?

_____

_____

3. Summarize their similarities and their differences.

Similarities: _____

_____

Differences: _____

_____

4. Make a judgment based on the information you compared and contrasted.

_____

_____

_____

_____

To review

↓

page
144

Visual Aids

Introducing Strategies

Good readers pay attention to the maps, charts, graphs, and tables that accompany encyclopedia articles. Good readers scan these **visual aids** to find out information quickly on a subject. As you read, use information in visual aids to make comparisons and to draw conclusions about a subject.

The pie graphs below show facts about how people are employed in China and Hong Kong.

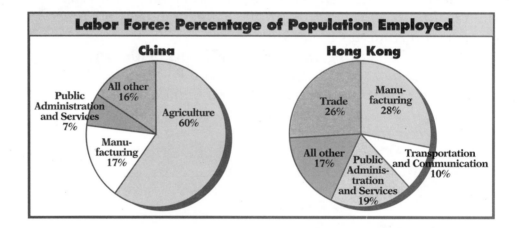

Reading the Encyclopedia Article

Reread the article "Hong Kong" on pages 133-138. As you read, circle the place names you come across. Locate these places on the map on page 138. Then complete the items below.

1. Why do you think the map was included with the article?

_____

_____

_____

2. How did the map help you understand the information given in the article?

_____

_____

_____

Practicing Visual Aids

A. Refer to the visual aids in the article "Hong Kong" to answer the questions below. On the lines, write the name of the visual aid you used to answer each question.

1. Compared to Hong Kong, about what percentage of the people in China live in cities?
   a. ten percent
   b. twenty-five percent
   c. about the same
   d. none of the above

_____

_____

2. The worth of which industry is the same for the gross national product in both China and Hong Kong?
   a. transportation
   b. trade
   c. construction
   d. none of the above

_____

_____

3. How many more people live in China than in Hong Kong?
   a. about half as many
   b. about twice as many
   c. about twenty times
   d. about 200 times

_____

_____

B. Review the visual aids in the article about Hong Kong. Write a sentence that summarizes the most important information you learned from each one.

_____

_____

_____

_____

_____

_____

_____

_____

_____

Applying *Visual Aids*

The items at the bottom of the page are based on the paragraph and bar graph immediately below. Read the paragraph and study the graph before answering the questions.

TRANSPORTATION: COSTLY TIME

Companies that manufacture goods are concerned about the cost of transporting those goods to consumers. The time it takes is important. The fastest means is also the most costly, which is why less than one half of one percent of freight in the United States goes by air. Most (about 40 percent) goes by rail.

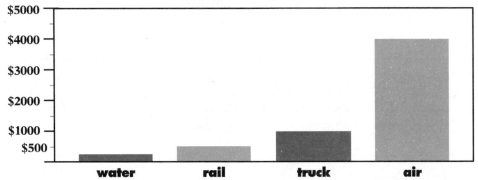

1. Compare the cost of shipping by truck and shipping by air.

_____

_____

2. Why do you think trains carry most of the freight in the United States?

_____

_____

To review
page
146

Shu Ching Chan grew up and received her college education in Hong Kong. After college, she worked for several years as an editor for large communication corporations before coming to the United States to complete a master's degree in radio and television. Now back in Hong Kong, she will be there for the 1997 takeover of that colony by China. As she notes in this portion of her encyclopedia article on Hong Kong, no one knows how smoothly the transition will go.

Hong Kong

by Shu Ching Chan

The notes in the margins on pages 133 and 134 show how one reader made judgments while comparing and contrasting information about Hong Kong and mainland China.

Hong Kong is a British colony. On July 1, 1997, it will become a Special Administrative Region (SAR) of the People's Republic of China (PRC). This is according to the Treaty of Nanking, which followed Britain's defeat of China in the First Opium War (1839-1842). The treaty gave the Chinese city of Hong Kong to Britain, with the agreement the city would be returned to China in 1997. Since the time of the treaty, many changes have occurred in China and Hong Kong that will affect the return of the city to Chinese rule.

◀ Hong Kong is a British colony now and it will soon become part of China again. But there are many differences today between Hong Kong and China.

In 1949, the People's Republic of China was established as a communist nation. Hong Kong, under British rule, remained capitalist. Under two such different systems, China and Hong Kong had little to do with each other. During the Cultural Revolution (1966-1976), the division became even greater, as China was completely shut off from the rest of the world.

◀ China has a communist government and has been isolated for many years from the rest of the world. Hong Kong has had a capitalist system and has not been isolated. These differences may be difficult to overcome.

During the Economic Reform, introduced in China in the 1980s, however, greater contact began to develop between China and Hong Kong. One reason for this was geographic. Hong Kong is the southern gateway to mainland China. Thus, it is through Hong Kong that China trades with the rest of the world. Another reason for improved relations between Hong Kong and China is economic. As China began to industrialize, the Hong Kong economy became more dependent upon trade with China. In addition, since many Western financial and business institutions already were well established in Hong Kong, business people in the city became involved in the development of businesses in China. Despite these improvements in Chinese-Hong Kong relations, many significant differences remain.

◀ It seems that differences declined in the 1980s. Hong Kong and China are close geographically. They had economic interests in common. Maybe these factors will make the takeover easier.

Hong Kong ■ **133**

Demographics (1992)		
	CHINA	HONG KONG
Population	1,165,888,000	5,799,000
Density (people per sq. mi.)	314.4	13,909
Percentage in Urban Areas	26.2	100
Percentage in Rural Areas	73.8	0

Fears about Communism

China is still communist, and most residents of Hong Kong fear the tactics of communist rulers worldwide. These fears were intensified by the Tiananmen Square incident in 1989. A peaceful rally for political reforms by students in the square of Beijing grew to a seven-week-long demonstration involving hundreds of thousands of people. In June, the demonstration was abruptly ended by forceful government action. Thousands of soldiers and tanks were sent into the square. Hundreds of demonstrators were killed as machine guns opened fire.

> China has a communist government, which uses force. The people in Hong Kong are concerned about this force.

▶ The senior leader of the communist party, Deng Xiaoping, has tried to relieve the fears about communism. He has promised that in Hong Kong there will be "no change for 50 years." The plan is for "one country, two systems."

Even with this promise, the fears have not gone away. As 1997 looms closer, many middle class and professional residents of Hong Kong are immigrating to other English-speaking countries—Canada, the United States, Australia, and Singapore. Hong Kong has been said to be suffering from a "brain drain."

Political, Economic, and Cultural Differences

Hong Kong began as part of China. Today, although 95 percent of its population is Chinese, many residents do not want to be influenced by the mainland Chinese. Hong Kong is now very different from its mother country politically, economically, and culturally. Even its demographics, or population statistics, are different. While most of the residents in Hong Kong, for instance, live in crowded urban areas, most in China live in rural areas.

> Here's another difference: China is more rural; Hong Kong is urban. I think that the treaty was signed so long ago that it shouldn't have to apply today.

▶

Politics

Hong Kong has a colonial government. The Hong Kong governor is appointed by the British government. A legislative council and an executive council exist, but elections and political parties are new to Hong Kong.

Compared with other Asian countries, the government of Hong Kong has been rather stable. Many residents of Hong Kong prefer to be "politically insensitive." This means they want to be left undisturbed by politics and government so that they can concentrate on working and making money.

Unlike other colonial countries in the Pacific, Hong Kong does not have natural resources to be exploited. The only significant resource is the hard-working population. So citizens of Hong Kong do not feel restricted by being colonial subjects. They enjoy the colony's economic prosperity and political stability.

Economics

As in other countries, the people of Hong Kong and China work in different kinds of occupations, which together make up each area's gross national product (GNP). The GNP is the value of the goods and services produced in one year. The table below shows how much those occupations are worth to Hong Kong and China's GNP. Obviously their economies are based on very different things.

China is an agricultural country. In 1992, 60 percent of the labor force worked in agriculture, with approximately 34 percent of the gross national product coming from their efforts. (For more information about the labor force in China and in Hong Kong, look at the pie graphs on page 130.) The economy in China is mainly

Write your own sidenotes as you read the rest of the article. Continue to make judgments as you compare and contrast the information about China and Hong Kong. Think about how the similarities and differences may affect the successful takeover of Hong Kong by China.

Gross National Product		
Industries	**China**	**Hong Kong**
Agriculture	34	*
Manufacturing	47	16
Construction	6	6
Transportation and Communication	7	9
Trade	6	23
Finance	*	30
Public Administration and Services	*	16

* less than 1 percent

planned by the government. Except in the big cities, the average living standard is much lower than it is in Hong Kong. In China, the average person earns $370.00 per year; in Hong Kong, the average earnings are $12,500.00 per year.

Hong Kong's economy is not based on agriculture. It is, above all, a place to do business. Hong Kong has become a major international center for finance, commerce, trade, and manufacturing. It has the world's second busiest port. Hong Kong has many successful industries and advanced means of communication. It has the greatest number of mobile phones in the world. The mobile phone is almost a trademark of the Hong Kong manager. Business people in Hong Kong are used to laissez-faire capitalism. That is, they are not used to government interference.

Culture

Culturally, Hong Kong is also very different from China. Hong Kong is greatly influenced by the West, meaning the United States and Europe. In China, however, Western influences are just beginning to have an effect.

English is the language of government, law, and international business in Hong Kong. Hollywood movies, English magazines, and English television programs appear everywhere. American fast-food chains abound. Music videos and news from American networks fill the shops, as do regional editions of major international newspapers and magazines.

The pace of life in Hong Kong is also much faster than it is in China. Hong Kong is a cosmopolitan, 24-hour city. During the day, business people from all over the world fill the offices and streets, taking advantage of Hong Kong's low tax rate and cheap goods. At night, thousands of restaurants stay open late, serving endless varieties of ethnic foods. Karaoke singing is a popular form of entertainment, as is dancing. Stores in Hong Kong, the "shopper's paradise," also stay open well into the night.

In China, only big cities like Beijing, Shanghai, and Guangzhou share the hectic pace and sophistication of Hong Kong. In these cities, Hong Kong business people feel somewhat at home. Elsewhere, the culture seems foreign to them.

Given the many differences between China and Hong Kong, the 1997 transition cannot be expected to occur without some problems. The hope is that the transition will serve as a model for the next one that will occur: the Chinese takeover of Macao, a Portuguese colony, in 1999. For now, however, people in Hong Kong are fond of saying, "Enjoy yourself today."

The Land

Hong Kong covers approximately 1,126 square miles of which 404 square miles are land situated in the South China Sea. Hong Kong includes more than 235 islands. Victoria, the capital, is on the north side of hilly Hong Kong Island. Kowloon, the largest urban area of Hong Kong, lies across the harbor on Kowloon peninsula. Hong Kong's largest region, called New Territories, lies behind Kowloon as a peninsula of mainland China.

Hong Kong Island is the most important island of the dependency. It is about 10 miles long and from 2 to 5 miles wide. The rice paddies of New Territories lie on a plain behind a line of hills adjacent to the urban area of Kowloon. A small river forms the border between Hong Kong and China. Trains between Kowloon and China stop at the border. Passengers must disembark and walk across a bridge to the railroad station on the other side.

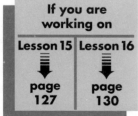

If you are working on

Lesson 15	Lesson 16
⬇	⬇
page 127	page 130

Venezuela

by Mary Ann Castronovo Fusco

Located on the northern coast of South America, Venezuela is the sixth-largest country on that continent. Its area is 352,143 square miles, which is a little more than two times the size of California. Early European explorers originally gave the name Venezuela, which means "Little Venice," to the area around Lake Maracaibo. They chose this name because the villages that they saw there reminded them of Venice, Italy.

Bounded on the north by the Caribbean Sea and the Atlantic Ocean, on the east by Guyana, on the south by Brazil, and on the west by Colombia, Venezuela is noted for its geographical diversity and beauty.

As you read, use the margins to make judgments as you note similarities and differences in climate, population, vegetation, and animal life in Venezuela's four regions.

Venezuela is a federal republic made up of 22 states, a federal district, and the federal dependencies of 72 islands in the Caribbean. The largest of the Venezuelan islands is Margarita, which is known for its pearls and fishing. It is also a popular tourist resort.

The Cities

The largest city in Venezuela is its capital, Caracas. Located about 3,000 feet (915 meters) above sea level in a beautiful valley in the shadow of Mt. Avila, it is the political, economic, and cultural center of the country. A sophisticated city of skyscrapers and universities, it is the birthplace of Simón Bolívar, the Great Liberator, who freed Venezuela and much of South America from Spanish rule. Other major cities include:

Maracaibo—Venezuela's second largest city, it is located on the western shore of Lake Maracaibo and is an oil center.

La Guaira—Located about 11 miles (18 km) from the capital, it is Venezuela's main port.

Barquisimeto—This fast-growing industrial city is located on the Pan-American Highway.

Maracay—This Spanish colonial town is the center of coffee and sugarcane production.

The People

Venezuela was sighted by Christopher Columbus in 1498 during his third voyage to the New World and was settled by Spaniards in the 1500s. After World War II, Venezuela attracted a great number of Italian emigrants searching for opportunity in the Americas. People from many cultural groups live there today, including Native Americans, African Americans, and European Americans. About 70 percent of its 21,665,000 people are mestizo—a mixture of Native American and European American heritages.

The Climate

Although Venezuela lies entirely in the tropical zone, temperatures and rainfall vary greatly, depending on altitude. Located south of the hurricane belt, Venezuela enjoys cool, dry trade winds from the northeast most of the year.

Venezuela has two seasons. *Verano,* or summer, is the dry season and goes from the end of November to early May. *Invierno,* or winter, is the rainy season, which lasts from the end of May to the middle of November. Because of its pleasant climate, Caracas is popularly called "the city of eternal spring."

Practicing Summarizing

A. Each pair of sentences below is based on the essay "Why—and How—the BIA Should Be Dissolved" on pages 143-145. Place a check in front of the sentence that states a main idea and could be used in a summary of the essay. Then explain your choices on the lines provided.

1. ___The BIA has had a negative impact on the lives of most Native Americans.

   ___The BIA has 12 regional centers in the United States.

   _____

   _____

2. ___The BIA originally was part of the Department of War.

   ___Because the BIA is set up to direct, not be a partner to, Native Americans, numerous frustrations arise.

   _____

   _____

3. ___The BIA is unnecessary because only Congress can make or regulate laws regarding Native Americans.

   ___The writer comes from the Pit River Nation.

   _____

   _____

4. ___The writer grew up in California.

   ___The writer believes that the BIA can be dissolved naturally.

   _____

   _____

B. Write a short paragraph that summarizes your own reaction to the ideas in the essay "Why—and How—the BIA Should Be Dissolved."

_____

_____

_____

_____

_____

The *Llanos* (Plains) or Orinoco Lowlands makes up almost one-third of the country. This grassland has numerous cattle ranches and is home to about 10% of the population. The Guiana Highlands, also called the Guayana, is densely forested. Although it is the largest of the four main regions, it only holds about 5% of the population.

Rivers and Lakes

Venezuela has more than 1,000 rivers. The most important one is the Orinoco, which is the second-longest river on the South American continent. Originating in the Guayana near the Brazilian border, the Orinoco flows 1,284 miles (2,066 km) before emptying into the Atlantic Ocean. The river and its 436 smaller branches drain most of the country.

Covering 5,217 square miles (13,512 square km), Venezuela's largest lake, Lake Maracaibo, is also the continent's largest. More than 130 rivers drain into it. Three-quarters of Venezuela's important petroleum reserves are located under the lake. Petroleum from the surrounding area has been one of the country's major exports since 1918. The lake's narrow exit to the Gulf of Venezuela is dredged to enable large oil tankers to reach the port of Maracaibo.

Plant and Animal Life

The vegetation of Venezuela varies with the landscape. Alpine shrubs called *frailejones* grow on the plateaus that rise more than 10,000 feet (3,048 meters). Lush tropical rain forests are found in the Maracaibo Basin, on the lower slopes of the Mérida Range, and in the Guiana Highlands, where hundreds of species of orchids also grow. Scrub and desert plants thrive along the dry Caribbean coast. In the *Llanos,* both short *yarafuá* grasses and taller *camelote* grasses can be found. In the Orinoco Delta there are swamp forests and mangrove thickets.

Venezuela's wildlife is not as plentiful as it once was, but it remains varied. Native animals include jaguars, pumas, ocelots, monkeys, sloths, anteaters, armadillos, peccaries, and otters. The rivers and streams are home to alligators, crocodiles, catfish, rays, electric eels, and piranhas. Red snapper, Spanish mackerel, bluefish, mullet, sardines, manatees, and dolphins swim in the coastal waters. Native reptiles include turtles, lizards, and several poisonous snakes. There is an abundance of tropical birds, such as parrots and macaws. Migratory birds that can be found in Venezuela's marshes and lagoons include ducks, storks, ibises, cranes, and herons.

Natural Resources

One of the world's ten largest oil producers, Venezuela has the largest known oil reserves outside the Middle East. In addition to its rich petroleum deposits, Venezuela has several other mineral resources, including iron ore, bauxite, gold, diamonds, coal, chrome, manganese, titanium, nickel, and copper.

Tourism

A land of great natural beauty, Venezuela has yet to reach its full potential as a tourist destination. To that end, the Venezuelan government is promoting the country's natural wonders and its opportunities for recreation. Adventure travel packages, such as encounters with native peoples, wildlife expeditions, rafting, Andean trekking, and bird watching, are also available.

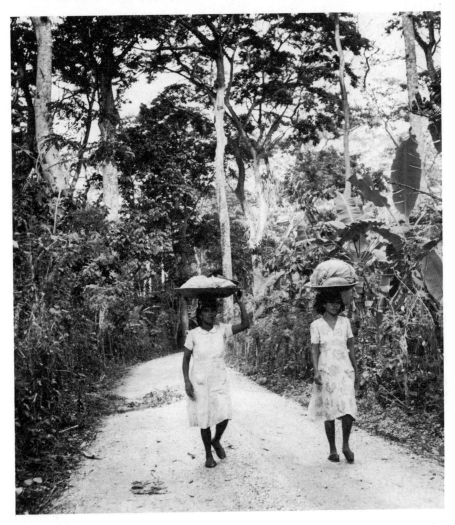

If you are working on

Lesson 15	Lesson 16
⬇	⬇
page 144	page 146

Reasons the BIA Is Unsatisfactory

To those who would argue that the BIA already functions as a partner, I present the following frustrations. All of these come from the fact that the BIA is set up to be our director, not our equal.

Conflicting Styles

The BIA is highly inaccessible to the people it is supposed to help. If we do get a chance to be heard by the BIA, we are not allowed to express ourselves in a way we find familiar and comfortable. Our way is to sit together, council-style. Together, we reach an agreement. The BIA way is to follow *Roberts' Rules of Order*. The meeting follows a chain of command, from the top down. We, of course, are on the bottom.

Conflicting Interests

The BIA is part of the Department of the Interior, which has authority over land, minerals, water, and other resources. Native Americans are especially concerned about the sacredness of these things. Reservations are practically the only spots left in the United States (besides state and federal parks) where land and minerals have been used wisely and preserved. Since our reservations are now under the Department of Interior's authority, the government is able to use our lands and resources to meet the needs of the majority.

In Washington, for example, the Department of Fish and Game has been at odds with Native Americans for years over fishing rights. At one time, an agreement was made regarding one river in the state. People fishing in the river were to pay attention to an "imaginary line" running down the middle of this river. Native Americans could fish on one side, and commercial companies could fish on the other side. Once, a Native American was accused by a game warden of fishing beyond the imaginary line. The fisherman's response, "I thought the imaginary line was over there," reveals some of the frustration with the rule. Native Americans find it hard to figure out rules that try to make nature "belong" to anyone. We do not understand how anyone can own the land we walk on any more than anyone could own the air we breathe.

Who Governs Native American Nations?

As Supreme Court Justice Ruth Ginsburg pointed out in 1993, any matter pertaining to Native American nations should *by law* be settled by Congress. According to the Constitution, the U.S. Congress is the only governing body that can make or regulate laws regarding our people. If this is so, the BIA is unnecessary.

However, contrary to the law, the Department of the Interior has organized our people into four groups, according to our willingness to work with the government:

- Federally Recognized: These groups receive federal benefits and assistance and are "on record" as a political group (like "Puerto Ricans" or "Vietnamese Americans").

- State Recognized: These groups receive state benefits and are "on record" as a political group.

- Terminated: These groups have formally cut off any ties with the federal government.

- Unrecognized: These groups do not receive state or federal benefits. They have not organized themselves in the way the Department of the Interior requires.

I come from the Pit River Nation, which is unrecognized. We feel that we are traditionally sovereign. This means that we govern ourselves in our traditional ways, through agreements among ourselves. We do not choose to waste our time with organizations like the BIA. In our way of thinking, only Congress has any legal power over us.

A Lack of Respect for our Ways

BIA officials suggest laws regarding the governing of our people to the Secretary of the Interior. Yet, these laws are suggested without consulting our people. The attitude is that the government knows the needs of the Native Americans. Laws are made, and Native Americans are pressured to accept them. Few, if any, Native Americans believe that this works well.

Change and Compromise

I don't think we have to eliminate the BIA. I think it can be phased out. Compromise between the BIA and Native American nations can result in a partnership that will help us attain our rightful legal standing in Congress. For this, we must wait patiently, drawing on the strength of our customs and traditions.

If you are working on

Lesson 15	Lesson 16
⬇	⬇
page 132	page 137

Reviewing *Visual Aids*

A. Reread the article on Venezuela on pages 139-143. As you read, circle any information given about the country's population. Use this information and create a pie graph below that compares the population of the four main regions.

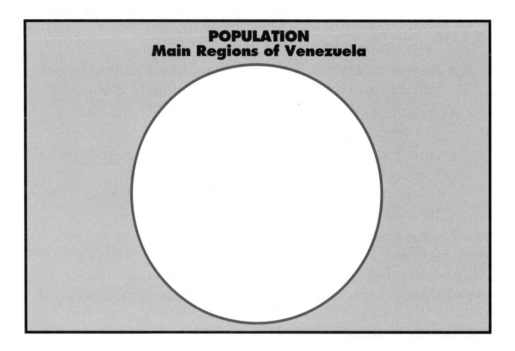

**POPULATION
Main Regions of Venezuela**

B. Do a survey of the students in your class. In the survey, compare future plans of the men and women. Create a visual aid that summarizes your findings.

_____

_____

_____

_____

_____

_____

_____

_____

_____

_____

Testing Visual Aids

A. Use the visual aids in "Venezuela" to complete the paragraph below. Choose an item from the column at the right that best completes each sentence.

Gina dreamed of traveling to Venezuela. From the United States, she'd like to take a freighter across the _____ to LaGuaira. She wouldn't have to travel far to explore the capital city. Then she'd go _____ to Lake Maracaibo. She'd like to take a boat down the _____, starting perhaps where the river itself divided Venezuela from _____. Gina wondered if, as she traveled the river through central Venezuela, she'd be able to see the _____ range to the southeast. At the end of the river, she wanted to explore the rain forest in the Orinoco Delta where _____ inches of rain fall in a year! "It's not only wet there," she remembered, "it's hot too—usually higher than _____ ° C." She sighed, "So much to do...."

1. 24
2. 80
3. Caribbean Sea
4. Colombia
5. east
6. Orinoco River
7. Pacavaima
8. west

B. Plan a trip to Venezuela. Look at the map on page 139. Choose an area you'd like to visit, then write an itinerary for the trip. Include what time of year you'd like to go, what you might see, what the weather might be like. Scan the article and the visual aids for information that will help you with your plans.

_____

_____

_____

_____

_____

_____

white. That is a reflection of our society as much as of the film industry."

When ethnicity is involved, producers should at least consult with the ethnic group for accuracy. In producing and directing *Dances with Wolves*, a movie about Native Americans, Kevin Costner consulted often with Native American authorities. He also cast Rodney Grant, a Native American actor, in a lead role. This extra work enhanced the success of the movie—it was named best picture of 1990!

Struggling for Parts

Asian Americans often are called the "model minority," the people whose hard work has helped them to achieve the "American dream." In reality, however, a majority of Asian Americans are struggling for equal status and recognition. This is especially true in the theater.

The casting director for *Miss Saigon*, Vincent G. Liff of the Johnson, Liff & Zerman casting agency, said that he was not able to find an Asian actor "suitable" for the role—one of more or less the right age who could act and sing. Mackintosh, the producer of the play, said a search was done worldwide for actors of Asian heritage to play the many different Asian roles. The search was indeed much publicized. However, it actually centered on casting the starring role of Kim, the young Asian woman. No actor but Jonathan Pryce was seriously considered for the leading male role. Therefore, there was not the sort of "good faith effort" Asians had expected.

In a perfect world, any artist should be able to play any role for which he or she is suited. Until that time arrives, however, artists of color must fight for the few roles that are culturally specific to them. In the diverse United States of today, equal opportunity in any area must not be denied. Besides, plays and movies can be made richer by the cultural background brought by Asians in leading roles.

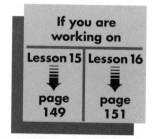

If you are
working on

Lesson 15	Lesson 16
⬇	⬇
page 149	page 151

Reviewing *Cause and Effect*

A. Read the essay "Why Asians Should Play Asian Roles" on pages 146-148. As you read, make notes in the margin when you identify a cause and effect relationship. Then use your sidenotes to complete the chart below.

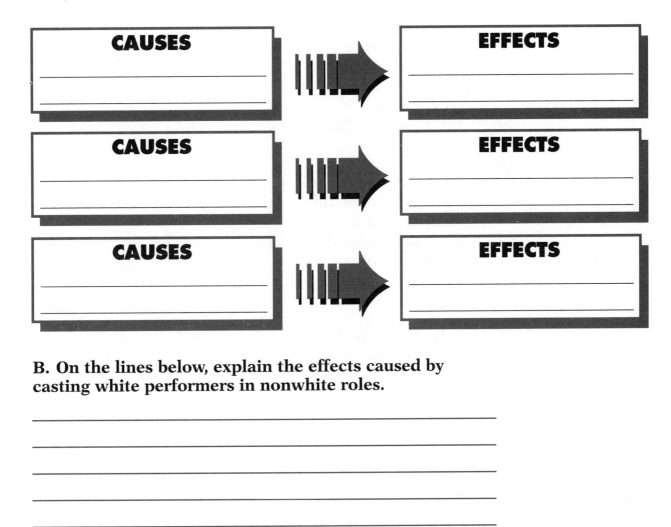

CAUSES → **EFFECTS**

CAUSES → **EFFECTS**

CAUSES → **EFFECTS**

B. On the lines below, explain the effects caused by casting white performers in nonwhite roles.

_____

_____

_____

_____

_____

_____

_____

_____

_____

_____

_____

Perfection

Schooled in rigid form.
Tuned as finely
as an instrument.
You view yourself
in the mirror,
a study
in perfection.

Your muscles flex.
Small movements
suggest emotion.
But whose feelings
do you show?
Whose ideas reflected
in your soul?

The form of dance is strict.
Each pose is measured, timed.
The arch of a foot,
the tilt of the head,
all give meaning.
To what?
Are you to know?

Schooled in rigid form.
Tuned as finely as
an instrument.
You are a tool
of a creator
whose vision
is not yours.

You long to be your own dance.
To put your heart
into your feet.
To break
with form and symmetry.
To feel the music
and fly free.

A. Use the poems and your notes to identify the best answer to each question.

1. What is the subject of both poems?
   a. why ballet is special
   b. the various forms of dance
   c. the importance of music
   d. how dance evokes feelings

2. How would you describe the mood of "Fast Dance"?
   a. exciting and free
   b. tense and mysterious
   c. calm and controlled
   d. silly and playful

3. Which line or lines in the first stanza of "Perfection" are an example of a simile?
   a. line 1
   b. lines 2 and 3
   c. lines 4 and 5
   d. lines 6 and 7

4. What point of view is expressed in "Fast Dance"?
   a. first person
   b. third person
   c. both first and third person
   d. no point of view

5. What word is a synonym for *symmetry* as it is used in "Perfection"?
   a. freedom
   b. irregularity
   c. balance
   d. uncertainty

6. What is one way in which both poems compare?
   a. both use first person
   b. both have five stanzas
   c. both are in free verse
   d. both use rhyme

B. How do you think the narrator of the first poem feels about dancing? How do you think the narrator of the second poem feels? Draw a conclusion about each narrator's feelings. Support each conclusion with details or words from the poem.

_____
_____
_____
_____
_____
_____
_____
_____
_____
_____

Testing Summarizing

A. Fill in the circle next to each statement that summarizes the main ideas in the essay "Why Asians Should Play Asian Roles" on pages 146-148. Then, on the lines provided, explain why you did or did not fill in the oval.

○ Marlon Brando played the role of Sakini in *The Teahouse of the August Moon.*

_____

_____

○ Historically, directors have used white actors and actresses to play Asians, but today one of the big issues in the entertainment industry is the casting of ethnic roles.

_____

_____

○ *Dances with Wolves* was named best picture of 1990.

_____

_____

○ By the year 2000, about 5 percent of the total U.S. population will be Asian American.

_____

_____

○ Asian American actors and actresses should have the opportunity to play Asian roles in movies and the theater.

_____

_____

B. Do you agree or disagree with the writer's position as stated in the essay? Why? Write a summary statement that expresses your own position on the casting of ethnic roles.

_____

_____

_____

_____

Book Test

PART 1: FICTION

Read the following scene from a play. Underline and draw circles to show relationships between words and ideas. Make notes in the margins as you read. Then use the selection and your notes to answer the questions on the next page.

CHARACTERS: TONY: a 14-year-old boy who is about to leave his pueblo to go to high school in a large city

ROXANNE: a 14-year-old girl from the same pueblo

SETTING: The shade of a large cottonwood tree. The tree is located along a river that runs through the pueblo in New Mexico. It is early fall, and the leaves on the tree are just beginning to turn a lovely golden color.

1 TONY: (*Gazing at river*) I can't believe we'll be in Santa Fe next week! What do you think school will be like?

3 ROXANNE: I don't know. It will be exciting, I'm sure. But also scary! (*She grimaces slightly.*) I'm not sure I'll feel comfortable living outside the pueblo. I mean, I'll miss my family during the week. I keep wondering what the city students will be like. Will I fit in?

8 TONY: (*Turning to* ROXANNE) I know what you mean. Sometimes I feel so secure. Our people have lived here for so many years. Each rock, each tree is special! Still, I long to go to a bigger school. (*He smiles gently at* ROXANNE *and then says hesitating,*) What if . . . the students don't understand our ways? Will we have to give up much of what we're used to?

14 ROXANNE: Maybe we should stay right here.

15 TONY: My family would never accept that decision. I know I would not be content either. (*He sighs.*)

16 ROXANNE: (*Touching* TONY's *hand gently*) Either way, where do we belong?

How Mexico City Compares to Other Cities in Mexico

City	Altitude (in feet)	Rainiest Months	Population
Acapulco	6	May-Oct.	409,335
Guadalajara*	5,140	June-Sept.	1,626,152
Merida	29	May-Oct.	424,529
Mexico City*	**7,575**	**June-Sept.**	**10,263,275**
Monterrey*	1,765	June, Sept., Oct.	1,090,009
Tijuana	2,552	July-Sept.	461,257
Veracruz	46	June-Oct.	305,456

* Figure does not include population of the suburbs.

Something for Everyone

4 Its historic attractions make Mexico City one of the most unique cities in the world. At the *Plaza of the Three Cultures* you'll find Aztec ruins and a Spanish colonial church set against the background of modern high-rise buildings. How about a visit to the *Zocalo*, the heart of the old city? Located on the very spot where the Aztecs built their Great Temple, this plaza is the site of the National Palace, a Spanish colonial building erected in the 1600's. Looking for fascinating museums and churches? The National Museum of Anthropology and the famous Basilica of Our Lady of Guadalupe will not disappoint you! And to round out your visit, why not take a trip to the ancient pyramids and temples north of the city?

5 But what about modern pleasures? Dining and dancing are at their best in Mexico City, and who can resist the adventure of shopping for handicrafts at the many shops and market places? Children will delight in lovely Chapultepec Park, and sporting fans can enjoy jai alai, soccer, and baseball. In addition, the city offers many excellent courses for golfing. So, the next time you have a taste for culture and entertainment, for the best of the past and the present — come to Mexico City!

Advertisement

A. Use the selection and your notes to identify the best answer to each question.

1. For what purpose was this advertorial written?

　　a. to entertain
　　b. to give historic facts
　　c. to "sell" Mexico City
　　d. to "sell" Mexican handicrafts

2. What words in this advertorial might appeal to readers' emotions?

　　a. temperature, altitude
　　b. capital, lake
　　c. Aztec, Spanish
　　d. colorful, fascinating

3. Which key word is specific to the subject of paragraph 3?

　　a. *climate*
　　b. *December*
　　c. *nights*
　　d. *summer*

4. What is the main idea of paragraph 4?

　　a. Mexico City is modern.
　　b. There are many historic sites.
　　c. The National Museum of Anthropology is famous.
　　d. Pyramids and temples lie north of the city

5. Considering that *Zocalo* means "base," which words in paragraph 4 reflect its meaning?

　　a. *on the very spot*
　　b. *this plaza*
　　c. *heart of the city*
　　d. *outdoor marketplace*

6. How does Mexico City compare in altitude to other cities on the chart?

　　a. Its altitude is 7,575 ft.
　　b. It has more people.
　　c. It is lower in altitude.
　　d. It is higher in altitude.

B. Write a paragraph based on the advertorial. In your paragraph, make three judgments about visiting Mexico City. Base your judgments on the information in the chart and in the advertorial.

_____

_____

_____

_____

_____

_____

_____

_____

_____

_____

_____

A. Use the selection and your notes to identify the best answer or answers to each question.

1. With which statement below would the writer of this editorial agree?
  a. We must all try to treat smokers more fairly.
  b. Smokers should not have their rights taken away.
  c. Smokers deserve no consideration at all.
  d. Smokers' rights are secondary to health.

2. Which of the following are key words related directly to the subject?
  a. *secondary smoke*
  b. *smoke-free workplace*
  c. *studies* and *research*
  d. *dangerous*

3. How would you describe the sentences in paragraph 3?
  a. mostly facts
  b. mostly opinion
  c. all facts
  d. all opinions

4. Which words give clues to the meaning of *ban* in the title and in paragraph 1?
  a. *smoke-free*
  b. *nonsmoking*
  c. *absence*
  d. *frequency*

5. According to the editorial, what are the results of NOT extending the smoking ban?
  a. more polluted air
  b. more lung cancer, emphysema, and high blood pressure
  c. loss of nonsmokers' rights
  d. loss of smokers' rights

6. Which persuasive technique does the last sentence in paragraph 2 illustrate?
  a. facts that appeal to reason
  b. storytelling to make a point
  c. statistics supporting the topic
  d. an opinion that appeals to emotion

B. Write a brief summary of the editorial. At the end of your summary, tell whether or not you think the writer's persuasive techniques were effective. Use examples to support your response.

_____

_____

_____

_____

_____

_____

_____

_____

_____

_____